FUNCTIONAL PROGRAMMING MASTERY:

FROM BEGINNER TO EXPERT IN MODERN PARADIGMS

Preface

Functional programming has steadily evolved from an academic curiosity to a mainstream paradigm influencing modern software development. The principles of immutability, pure functions, and declarative coding have found their way into programming languages, shaping the way developers write efficient, maintainable, and scalable software. This book serves as a comprehensive introduction to functional programming, guiding both beginners and experienced developers through its foundational concepts, techniques, and real-world applications.

In **Chapter 1**, we introduce the functional paradigm, tracing its origins, contrasting it with imperative programming, and discussing its advantages and challenges. **Chapter 2** delves into the core principles of functional programming, including pure functions, immutability, and higher-order functions. **Chapter 3** explores functional techniques such as function composition, currying, recursion, and lazy evaluation.

Data handling in functional programming is covered in **Chapter 4**, where we discuss functional data structures, error handling with monads, and managing side effects using pure functional approaches. **Chapter 5** expands on functional paradigms, explaining algebraic data types, monads, and category theory fundamentals.

A practical exploration of functional programming in various languages—including JavaScript, Python, Scala, and Haskell—is provided in **Chapter 6**. The real-world impact of functional programming is examined in **Chapter 7**, which discusses its use in web development, machine learning, distributed systems, reactive programming, and even game development.

For those looking to deepen their knowledge, **Chapter 8** introduces advanced topics such as type inference, functional state management, and domain-specific languages. **Chapter 9** provides best practices for writing clean, performant functional code, along with strategies for debugging, testing, and optimizing large-scale functional applications.

Finally, **Chapter 10** looks toward the future, highlighting emerging trends, the increasing adoption of functional programming in industry, and its role in AI and blockchain. The book concludes with a set of appendices in **Chapter 11**, offering a glossary, additional resources, and sample projects to solidify learning.

Whether you are a developer looking to adopt functional programming for the first time or an experienced programmer seeking to refine your expertise, this book provides a structured and practical approach to mastering functional programming.

Table of Contents

Chapter 1: Introduction to Functional Programming

Understanding the Functional Paradigm

Functional programming is a declarative programming paradigm that treats computation as the evaluation of mathematical functions, avoiding changing states and mutable data. It is rooted in lambda calculus, a formal system for expressing computation based on function abstraction and application.

At its core, functional programming promotes a programming style that is predictable, modular, and composable. Instead of modifying variables, functional programs rely on immutable data and pure functions, which always return the same output given the same input.

Imperative vs. Declarative Approaches

To understand functional programming, it is essential to contrast it with imperative programming. In an imperative paradigm, a programmer specifies step-by-step instructions to change the state of a program. This includes modifying variables, using loops, and handling mutable data.

In contrast, the declarative nature of functional programming allows developers to express *what* should be computed rather than *how*. For example, consider summing an array imperatively versus functionally:

Imperative Approach (JavaScript):

```javascript
let sum = 0;
let numbers = [1, 2, 3, 4, 5];
for (let i = 0; i < numbers.length; i++) {
    sum += numbers[i];
}
console.log(sum); // Output: 15
```

Functional Approach (JavaScript):

```javascript
const numbers = [1, 2, 3, 4, 5];
const sum = numbers.reduce((acc, num) => acc + num, 0);
console.log(sum); // Output: 15
```

The functional version is more concise, eliminating state mutations and explicitly defining the operation using reduce, which expresses the summation as a function application.

Key Characteristics of Functional Programming

Pure   **Functions**

A pure function is a function where the output is solely determined by the input, with no side effects. This property makes functions predictable and easier to test.

Example   **of**   **a**   **Pure**   **Function**   **(Python):**

python

```python
def add(a, b):
    return a + b
print(add(2, 3))   # Output: 5
```

1. Here, add(2, 3) will always return 5, no matter when or where it is called.

Immutability

In functional programming, data structures are immutable, meaning they cannot be modified after creation. Instead of modifying an array or object, new versions are created.

Example   **of**   **Immutability**   **(JavaScript):**

javascript

```javascript
const numbers = [1, 2, 3];
const newNumbers = [...numbers, 4]; // Creates a new array instead of
modifying the original
console.log(newNumbers); // Output: [1, 2, 3, 4]
```

2.

First-Class   **Functions**   **and**   **Higher-Order**   **Functions**

Functions in functional programming can be treated as first-class citizens, meaning they can be assigned to variables, passed as arguments, and returned from other functions.

Example   **of**   **a**   **Higher-Order**   **Function**   **(JavaScript):**

javascript

```javascript
function greet(name) {
    return function(message) {
        return `${message}, ${name}!`;
    };
}

const greetJohn = greet("John");
console.log(greetJohn("Hello")); // Output: Hello, John!
```

3.

Function **Composition**

Function composition is the process of combining multiple functions to create new functionality. This avoids deep nesting and makes code more modular.

Example of Function Composition (JavaScript):

javascript

```
const toUpperCase = str => str.toUpperCase();
const exclaim = str => `${str}!`;
const shout = str => exclaim(toUpperCase(str));

console.log(shout("hello")); // Output: HELLO!
```

4.

Referential **Transparency**

Referential transparency means that a function call can be replaced with its result without changing the program's behavior. This allows for easier reasoning and optimization techniques like memoization.

Example of Referential Transparency (Haskell):

haskell

```
square x = x * x
main = print (square 4) -- Always outputs 16
```

5.

Benefits of Functional Programming

- **Modularity:** Functions can be composed and reused across different parts of a program.
- **Predictability:** Pure functions make it easier to reason about code and avoid unexpected side effects.
- **Parallelism and Concurrency:** Immutability and pure functions enable safe concurrent execution.
- **Testability:** Pure functions and immutability simplify unit testing and debugging.

Challenges of Functional Programming

- **Learning Curve:** Developers accustomed to imperative programming might find functional paradigms challenging initially.
- **Performance Overhead:** Some functional techniques (e.g., recursion over loops) can introduce performance inefficiencies.
- **State Management:** Managing application state functionally requires different strategies compared to object-oriented approaches.

Overview of Modern Functional Programming Languages

Several languages embrace functional programming, either fully or as part of a multi-paradigm approach:

- **Haskell:** A purely functional language with strong static typing.
- **Scala:** Combines functional and object-oriented programming.
- **Elixir:** A functional language designed for concurrent applications.
- **Clojure:** A Lisp-based language with functional features.
- **JavaScript (ES6+):** Supports functional concepts such as first-class functions, higher-order functions, and immutability.
- **Python:** While primarily imperative, Python includes functional features such as `map`, `filter`, and `reduce`.

Conclusion

Functional programming presents a powerful approach to software development that prioritizes composability, immutability, and pure functions. While it introduces a different mindset from imperative programming, the benefits of maintainability, scalability, and testability make it an essential paradigm for modern developers. The following chapters will explore its core principles, techniques, and applications in greater depth.

History and Evolution of Functional Programming

Functional programming (FP) has a deep-rooted history that spans over seven decades, tracing its origins back to the early days of computer science. While it was initially an academic discipline, FP has grown into a widely used paradigm influencing modern programming languages and software development methodologies. Understanding its evolution provides valuable insight into the principles and philosophies that shape functional programming today.

The Mathematical Foundations: Lambda Calculus

The foundation of functional programming lies in **lambda calculus**, a formal system developed by **Alonzo Church** in the 1930s. Lambda calculus is a system of mathematical notation for expressing computation using function abstraction and application.

```
λx. x + 1
```

This represents an anonymous function that takes an argument x and returns $x + 1$. Functions in lambda calculus are **first-class citizens**, meaning they can be passed as arguments, returned from other functions, and composed together—concepts that remain central to modern functional programming.

Lambda calculus provided a theoretical framework that later influenced the development of functional programming languages and formal verification systems in computer science.

The Early Functional Programming Languages

The first functional programming languages emerged in the late 1950s and early 1960s, taking inspiration from lambda calculus and its formal approach to computation.

Lisp: The Pioneer of Functional Programming

Lisp (LISt Processing language), developed by **John McCarthy** in 1958, is one of the earliest programming languages to incorporate functional principles. Lisp introduced:

- **First-class functions** (functions as values)
- **Recursion** as a fundamental control structure
- **Garbage collection** to manage memory automatically

Lisp's syntax is minimalistic, using **s-expressions** to represent both code and data. An example of a recursive factorial function in Lisp:

```
(defun factorial (n)
  (if (<= n 1)
      1
      (* n (factorial (- n 1)))))
```

Lisp became popular in artificial intelligence research and academic circles, influencing many later languages.

ML and the Birth of Strongly Typed Functional Programming

In the 1970s, **Robin Milner** developed **ML (MetaLanguage)**, introducing **static type inference** and **pattern matching**. ML played a significant role in formalizing type systems and inspired many later languages, including **OCaml** and **F#**.

An ML function to compute the sum of a list:

```
fun sum [] = 0
  | sum (x::xs) = x + sum xs;
```

ML's strict type system and immutability principles contributed to the safety and reliability of software written in functional languages.

Haskell: The Pure Functional Language

The late 1980s and early 1990s saw the development of **Haskell**, a purely functional language emphasizing **lazy evaluation** and **type safety**. Named after **Haskell Curry**, a mathematician known for work in combinatory logic, Haskell enforces **pure functions**—functions that avoid side effects and always produce the same output for the same input.

A simple Haskell function to compute Fibonacci numbers:

```
fib :: Int -> Int
fib 0 = 0
fib 1 = 1
fib n = fib (n - 1) + fib (n - 2)
```

Haskell introduced **monads**, which provide a way to handle **side effects** in pure functional programming. Monads became a central abstraction in Haskell for dealing with **I/O, state management, and error handling**.

Functional Programming in Multi-Paradigm Languages

By the early 2000s, mainstream programming languages began incorporating functional programming concepts. **JavaScript (ES6+), Python, Java, C#, and Kotlin** introduced first-class functions, higher-order functions, and functional data structures.

JavaScript: Embracing Functional Programming

With the rise of **JavaScript ES6+**, functional programming became more accessible to a broader audience. JavaScript supports **first-class functions**, **higher-order functions**, and **functional array methods** like map, filter, and reduce.

Example of function composition in JavaScript:

```
const toUpper = str => str.toUpperCase();
const exclaim = str => `${str}!`;
const shout = str => exclaim(toUpper(str));

console.log(shout("hello")); // Output: "HELLO!"
```

The adoption of **React** and **Redux** further popularized **immutability** and **pure functions**, reinforcing functional programming in web development.

Python: Functional Features in an Imperative World

Although Python is primarily an **imperative** language, it includes several functional programming features:

- **Lambda expressions** for defining anonymous functions
- **Higher-order functions** like map(), filter(), and reduce()
- **List comprehensions** that resemble functional transformations

Example of functional programming in Python:

```
numbers = [1, 2, 3, 4, 5]
squared = list(map(lambda x: x ** 2, numbers))
print(squared)  # Output: [1, 4, 9, 16, 25]
```

Functional Features in Java and C#

Languages like **Java** and **C#** have incorporated functional programming through **lambda expressions**, **stream processing**, and **immutability**.

Example of Java streams for functional data transformation:

```
List<Integer> numbers = Arrays.asList(1, 2, 3, 4, 5);
List<Integer> squared = numbers.stream()
                              .map(n -> n * n)
                              .collect(Collectors.toList());
System.out.println(squared); // Output: [1, 4, 9, 16, 25]
```

These additions enable Java and C# developers to leverage functional programming in **multi-threaded and parallel computing** environments.

The Rise of Functional Programming in Industry

Functional programming has gained traction in industry due to its benefits in **concurrent computing, big data processing, and fault tolerance**. Prominent technologies influenced by functional programming include:

- **Scala**: Used in **Apache Spark** for distributed data processing
- **Elixir**: Built on **Erlang**, known for scalable and fault-tolerant applications
- **F#**: A functional-first language for .NET, popular in finance and scientific computing

Example of Elixir's pattern matching:

```
defmodule Math do
  def factorial(0), do: 1
  def factorial(n), do: n * factorial(n - 1)
end
```

Functional programming is widely adopted in **web development (React, Elm, ReasonML)**, **machine learning (TensorFlow, PyTorch)**, and **blockchain (smart contract languages like Solidity and Plutus)**.

The Future of Functional Programming

The increasing complexity of software systems has driven the need for **immutability, parallelism, and reliability**—all strengths of functional programming. Future trends include:

- **Wider adoption of purely functional languages** like Haskell and Elm
- **Hybrid approaches** in languages like Rust, Go, and Swift
- **Functional programming in AI and blockchain**
- **Better tooling and language ergonomics** to simplify FP adoption

As software development continues to evolve, functional programming will remain a powerful paradigm, shaping the way developers build scalable and maintainable applications.

Conclusion

From its roots in lambda calculus to its modern-day applications in large-scale software, functional programming has evolved significantly. Languages like Lisp, ML, and Haskell pioneered the field, while mainstream languages like JavaScript, Python, and Java have integrated functional paradigms. Today, functional programming is a vital tool in developing high-performance, concurrent, and maintainable applications. The journey of functional programming is far from over, and its principles continue to influence the future of software development.

Key Differences Between Functional and Imperative Programming

Functional programming (FP) and imperative programming (IP) represent two fundamentally different approaches to writing software. While functional programming focuses on immutability, pure functions, and declarative constructs, imperative programming emphasizes step-by-step state modifications and control flow. Understanding their differences is crucial for developers transitioning between these paradigms or incorporating functional concepts into existing imperative codebases.

Programming Paradigms: An Overview

A **programming paradigm** is a style or approach to solving problems using a programming language. The two major paradigms under discussion are:

1. **Imperative Programming**
   - Defines a sequence of instructions that change the program's state.
   - Uses **variables**, **loops**, and **mutable data structures**.
   - Examples: C, Java (pre-Java 8), Python (imperative style), and JavaScript (before ES6 functional features).
2. **Functional Programming**
   - Focuses on **pure functions** with no side effects.
   - Treats computation as the evaluation of mathematical functions.
   - Uses **immutable data structures** and avoids shared state.
   - Examples: Haskell, Lisp, Scala, and JavaScript (ES6+ with functional methods).

Comparison of Functional and Imperative Approaches

1. State Management: Mutable vs. Immutable State

One of the biggest differences between imperative and functional programming is how they handle state.

- **Imperative Programming:** Modifies state using variables, often causing side effects.
- **Functional Programming:** Avoids modifying state and instead returns new data.

Example: Mutable State in Imperative Programming (Python)

```python
counter = 0  # Mutable variable

def increment():
    global counter  # Modify global state
    counter += 1
    return counter

print(increment())  # Output: 1
print(increment())  # Output: 2
```

The function `increment()` modifies a global variable, making its behavior **dependent on external state**.

Example: Immutable State in Functional Programming (Python)

```python
def increment(counter):
    return counter + 1  # Returns a new value instead of modifying state

print(increment(0))  # Output: 1
print(increment(1))  # Output: 2
```

Here, `increment()` does not modify `counter`; it simply returns a new value.

2. Control Flow: Loops vs. Recursion

Imperative programming typically uses loops (`for`, `while`), while functional programming prefers recursion.

Imperative Approach: Using Loops (JavaScript)

```javascript
function factorial(n) {
    let result = 1;
    for (let i = 1; i <= n; i++) {
        result *= i;
    }
    return result;
}

console.log(factorial(5)); // Output: 120
```

Functional Approach: Using Recursion (JavaScript)

```javascript
function factorial(n) {
    return n === 0 ? 1 : n * factorial(n - 1);
}

console.log(factorial(5)); // Output: 120
```

Recursion eliminates mutable variables, making functions easier to reason about, though it requires optimization techniques like **tail recursion** for efficiency.

3. Function Behavior: Side Effects vs. Pure Functions

A function has **side effects** if it modifies external state, performs I/O, or changes a global variable.

Imperative Function with Side Effects (Python)

```python
def append_to_list(lst, value):
    lst.append(value)  # Modifies external state
    return lst

my_list = [1, 2, 3]
print(append_to_list(my_list, 4))  # Output: [1, 2, 3, 4]
print(my_list)  # External list is modified
```

Functional Approach: Pure Function (Python)

```python
def append_to_list(lst, value):
```

```
    return lst + [value]   # Returns a new list instead of modifying
existing one

my_list = [1, 2, 3]
print(append_to_list(my_list, 4))  # Output: [1, 2, 3, 4]
print(my_list)  # Output: [1, 2, 3] (original list remains unchanged)
```

In functional programming, **pure functions** ensure referential transparency, making reasoning and debugging easier.

4. Data Manipulation: Mutation vs. Transformation

Functional programming prefers **data transformations** using functions like map, filter, and reduce.

Imperative Approach: Modifying an Array (JavaScript)

```
let numbers = [1, 2, 3, 4];
for (let i = 0; i < numbers.length; i++) {
    numbers[i] *= 2;
}
console.log(numbers); // Output: [2, 4, 6, 8]
```

Functional Approach: Transforming an Array (JavaScript)

```
const numbers = [1, 2, 3, 4];
const doubled = numbers.map(n => n * 2);
console.log(doubled); // Output: [2, 4, 6, 8]
```

The functional approach keeps numbers **unchanged**, returning a new array instead.

5. Concurrency: Shared State vs. Isolation

Imperative programs often struggle with **concurrency** because of shared mutable state, leading to race conditions.

Functional programming avoids these issues by emphasizing **immutability and stateless functions**, making parallel execution easier.

Example: Thread-Safe Functional Computation (Scala)

```
val numbers = List(1, 2, 3, 4)
val doubled = numbers.par.map(_ * 2)   // Parallel processing using
immutable data
println(doubled) // Output: [2, 4, 6, 8]
```

Since **immutable structures cannot be modified**, functions are naturally thread-safe.

Hybrid Approaches: Mixing Functional and Imperative Styles

Many modern languages adopt a **multi-paradigm** approach, combining both imperative and functional concepts.

Example: JavaScript Mixing Both Styles

```
let numbers = [1, 2, 3, 4];

// Imperative
let sum = 0;
for (let num of numbers) {
    sum += num;
}

// Functional
let sumFunctional = numbers.reduce((acc, num) => acc + num, 0);

console.log(sum);   // Output: 10
console.log(sumFunctional);   // Output: 10
```

While `reduce()` provides a more **declarative** solution, both approaches achieve the same result.

Summary of Differences

Feature	Imperative Programming	Functional Programming
State Management	Mutable state, variables modified directly	Immutable state, new values returned
Control Flow	Loops (`for`, `while`)	Recursion, function calls

Function Behavior	Side effects allowed	Pure functions, no side effects
Data Handling	Mutation of objects	Transformation via map, filter, reduce
Concurrency	Issues with shared state	Thread-safe due to immutability
Code Readability	Explicit steps and instructions	Declarative, focuses on "what" rather than "how"

Conclusion

Functional and imperative programming offer distinct approaches to writing code. While imperative programming is more natural for beginners and aligns with how computers execute instructions, functional programming provides powerful abstractions that make code **more predictable, testable, and scalable**. Understanding both paradigms allows developers to choose the right approach for their specific needs, whether writing low-level systems or designing scalable, concurrent applications.

Benefits and Challenges of Functional Programming

Functional programming (FP) has gained significant traction in modern software development due to its numerous advantages, such as improved code maintainability, better modularity, and safer concurrency. However, like any paradigm, it also presents challenges that developers must consider when deciding to adopt it. This section explores the key benefits and challenges of functional programming, providing insights into how and when it should be used.

Benefits of Functional Programming

1. Code Maintainability and Readability

One of the most significant benefits of functional programming is its emphasis on **pure functions and immutability**, which lead to more **predictable** and **easier-to-read** code. Functional programs tend to be modular, reducing complexity.

Example: Imperative vs. Functional Code for Filtering Even Numbers (JavaScript)

Imperative Approach:

```
let numbers = [1, 2, 3, 4, 5, 6];
let evens = [];
for (let i = 0; i < numbers.length; i++) {
```

```
    if (numbers[i] % 2 === 0) {
        evens.push(numbers[i]);
    }
}
console.log(evens); // Output: [2, 4, 6]
```

Functional Approach:

```
const numbers = [1, 2, 3, 4, 5, 6];
const evens = numbers.filter(n => n % 2 === 0);
console.log(evens); // Output: [2, 4, 6]
```

In the functional approach, **the intent is clear**: apply a filtering function to extract even numbers. There is **no need to manage loop indices** or modify an external variable, making it easier to maintain.

2. Immutability Leads to Fewer Bugs

In functional programming, data structures are **immutable**, meaning they cannot be modified after creation. Instead of changing existing data, new values are created, reducing the likelihood of unintended side effects.

Example: Avoiding Mutation (Python)

```
def add_element(original_list, element):
    return original_list + [element]  # Returns a new list

nums = [1, 2, 3]
new_nums = add_element(nums, 4)

print(nums)      # Output: [1, 2, 3] (original list remains unchanged)
print(new_nums)  # Output: [1, 2, 3, 4]
```

Since nums remains unchanged, other functions using it are not accidentally affected.

3. Easier Debugging and Testing

Because **pure functions** always return the same output given the same input and have no side effects, debugging and testing become much simpler. Functional programs avoid **hidden state changes**, making it easier to isolate and fix bugs.

Example: Pure Function for Squaring a Number (JavaScript)

```
function square(x) {
    return x * x;
}

console.log(square(4));   // Output: 16
console.log(square(4));   // Output: 16 (Always predictable)
```

Since square(4) always returns 16, it can be tested **without any dependency on external state**.

4. Better Modularity and Reusability

Functional programming promotes **function composition**, where small, reusable functions are combined to perform complex operations.

Example: Composing Functions in JavaScript

```
const toUpperCase = str => str.toUpperCase();
const addExclamation = str => str + "!";
const shout = str => addExclamation(toUpperCase(str));

console.log(shout("hello")); // Output: "HELLO!"
```

Each function performs a single operation, making it easier to test, reuse, and compose.

5. Safer Concurrency and Parallelism

Functional programming avoids **shared mutable state**, which makes concurrent programming significantly safer. Since data is **immutable**, there are no race conditions caused by multiple threads modifying the same variables.

Example: Safe Parallel Processing in Scala

```
val numbers = List(1, 2, 3, 4)
val doubled = numbers.par.map(_ * 2)   // Parallel execution
println(doubled) // Output: [2, 4, 6, 8]
```

By default, the **immutable nature** of functional structures ensures that parallel operations **do not cause data corruption**.

6. Declarative Code Reduces Complexity

Functional programming emphasizes **what** should be done rather than **how**. This declarative nature makes code more intuitive and less error-prone.

Example: Imperative vs. Functional Approach to Summing an Array (Python)

Imperative Approach:

```python
numbers = [1, 2, 3, 4, 5]
sum_total = 0
for num in numbers:
    sum_total += num
print(sum_total)  # Output: 15
```

Functional Approach:

```python
numbers = [1, 2, 3, 4, 5]
sum_total = sum(numbers)
print(sum_total)  # Output: 15
```

The functional approach **eliminates boilerplate code**, making it easier to understand at a glance.

Challenges of Functional Programming

Despite its benefits, functional programming has challenges that can make it difficult to adopt in certain scenarios.

1. Steeper Learning Curve

Functional programming requires a **paradigm shift**, especially for developers accustomed to imperative or object-oriented programming. Concepts like **recursion, higher-order functions, and monads** can be difficult to grasp initially.

Example: Recursion vs. Loops (JavaScript)

Imperative Approach:

```javascript
function factorial(n) {
    let result = 1;
    for (let i = 1; i <= n; i++) {
        result *= i;
```

```
    }
    return result;
}
```

Functional Approach (Recursion):

```
function factorial(n) {
    return n === 0 ? 1 : n * factorial(n - 1);
}
```

Many developers find recursion **less intuitive** than loops.

2. Performance Overhead Due to Immutability

Creating **new objects instead of modifying existing ones** can lead to performance issues in memory-intensive applications.

Example: Copying Lists Instead of Modifying in Python

```
nums = [1, 2, 3]
new_nums = nums + [4]   # Creates a new list, rather than modifying
the original
```

While this prevents side effects, it **increases memory usage**.

3. Recursion Can Lead to Stack Overflow

Since functional programming encourages recursion over loops, it can lead to **stack overflow** if not optimized with **tail recursion**.

Example: Inefficient Recursion (Python)

```
def factorial(n):
    if n == 0:
        return 1
    return n * factorial(n - 1)

print(factorial(1000))  # StackOverflowError!
```

4. Limited Libraries and Frameworks

Many popular libraries and frameworks are designed for **imperative and object-oriented programming**, making functional programming **harder to integrate** in some ecosystems.

5. Debugging Higher-Order Functions Can Be Difficult

While functional programming simplifies **unit testing**, debugging **composed functions and monads** can be complex.

```
const        processData       =        data        =>
data.map(toUpperCase).map(addExclamation);
```

Tracking errors inside **composed functions** can be challenging.

Conclusion

Functional programming offers numerous advantages, including **better maintainability, modularity, safer concurrency, and declarative coding**. However, it also presents **challenges** such as **steeper learning curves, performance concerns, and debugging complexities**. The choice to adopt functional programming depends on the specific requirements of the project, the team's familiarity with the paradigm, and the available tooling. Many modern languages now incorporate functional features, enabling developers to **leverage the best of both functional and imperative programming** for writing clean, efficient, and maintainable software.

Overview of Modern Functional Programming Languages

Functional programming (FP) has evolved significantly over the past few decades, with many modern programming languages incorporating functional concepts or being designed entirely around functional principles. Some languages, such as Haskell, are **purely functional**, while others, like JavaScript and Python, are **multi-paradigm**, allowing a mix of functional, imperative, and object-oriented programming.

This section explores key modern functional programming languages, their features, and their influence on software development.

Pure Functional Programming Languages

Some languages are designed to be **purely functional**, meaning they enforce immutability, pure functions, and declarative programming by default.

1. Haskell: The Purest Functional Language

Haskell is one of the most well-known **pure functional** programming languages. It enforces **lazy evaluation**, **strong static typing**, and **pure functions**, making it a favorite for academic research, financial modeling, and distributed systems.

Key Features:

- **Pure functions** (side-effect-free)
- **Lazy evaluation** (expressions are evaluated only when needed)
- **Monads** (used for handling side effects)
- **Type inference** (no need to specify types explicitly)

Example: Fibonacci Sequence in Haskell

```
fib :: Int -> Int
fib 0 = 0
fib 1 = 1
fib n = fib (n - 1) + fib (n - 2)

main = print (fib 10) -- Output: 55
```

Haskell ensures immutability and avoids shared mutable state, making it ideal for **parallel computing and concurrency**.

2. Elm: Functional Web Development

Elm is a **functional language for front-end development**, designed to build robust, maintainable web applications.

Key Features:

- **No runtime exceptions** (strong type system)
- **Immutable state** (helps with debugging)
- **Compiles to JavaScript** (efficient front-end rendering)

Example: A Simple Elm Program

```
module Main exposing (main)

import Html exposing (text)

main = text "Hello, Functional World!"
```

Elm's architecture heavily influences **Redux** in JavaScript, promoting unidirectional data flow and immutability.

3. PureScript: Functional JavaScript Alternative

PureScript is similar to Haskell but compiles to JavaScript, making it useful for **front-end and back-end** web development.

Example: Mapping Over a List in PureScript

```
doubleNumbers = map (\x -> x * 2) [1, 2, 3, 4]
```

PureScript provides **strong type safety**, preventing common JavaScript runtime errors.

Multi-Paradigm Languages with Functional Features

Many mainstream languages, originally designed for imperative or object-oriented programming, have integrated functional programming features.

4. JavaScript: The Functional Web Language

JavaScript has transformed into a **functional-friendly** language with ES6+ enhancements, including **arrow functions, higher-order functions, and immutability**.

Key Functional Features in JavaScript:

- **First-class functions** (functions are treated as variables)
- **Higher-order functions** (functions can take other functions as arguments)
- **Immutable data structures** (via libraries like Immutable.js)

Example: Functional Array Manipulation

```
const numbers = [1, 2, 3, 4, 5];
const squared = numbers.map(n => n * n);
console.log(squared); // Output: [1, 4, 9, 16, 25]
```

JavaScript frameworks like **React** rely heavily on functional programming principles, such as **pure functions and immutability**.

5. Python: Functional Capabilities in a General-Purpose Language

Python supports functional programming via built-in functions like `map()`, `filter()`, `reduce()`, and lambda expressions.

Example: Functional Approach in Python

```
numbers = [1, 2, 3, 4, 5]
squared = list(map(lambda x: x ** 2, numbers))
print(squared)  # Output: [1, 4, 9, 16, 25]
```

Although Python is primarily imperative, libraries like **PyFunctional** and **Toolz** enhance its functional capabilities.

6. Scala: A Hybrid Functional and Object-Oriented Language

Scala combines **functional programming with object-oriented principles**, making it popular in **big data processing and distributed computing**.

Key Functional Features in Scala:

- **Pattern matching** (like Haskell)
- **Immutable collections** (encourages functional style)
- **Concurrency support** (via Akka framework)

Example: Functional List Processing in Scala

```
val numbers = List(1, 2, 3, 4, 5)
val doubled = numbers.map(_ * 2)
println(doubled) // Output: [2, 4, 6, 8, 10]
```

Scala is widely used in **Apache Spark** for processing large-scale data.

7. Kotlin: Functional Features in a Modern JVM Language

Kotlin, designed as an alternative to Java, incorporates functional programming through **lambda expressions, higher-order functions, and immutability**.

Example: Functional Programming in Kotlin

```
val numbers = listOf(1, 2, 3, 4, 5)
val doubled = numbers.map { it * 2 }
println(doubled) // Output: [2, 4, 6, 8, 10]
```

Kotlin's functional features make it **concise, expressive, and safe** for modern development.

8. C#: Functional Extensions to an Object-Oriented Language

C# has added **functional programming support** through LINQ, lambda expressions, and immutable data structures.

Example: Using LINQ in C#

```
var numbers = new List<int> { 1, 2, 3, 4, 5 };
var doubled = numbers.Select(n => n * 2);
Console.WriteLine(string.Join(", ", doubled)); // Output: 2, 4, 6, 8,
10
```

Functional programming in C# enhances **data transformations, concurrency, and composability**.

Functional Programming in Industry

Functional programming is widely used in industry, particularly in **high-performance computing, web development, machine learning, and blockchain**.

1. Functional Programming in Web Development

- **React (JavaScript):** Uses **pure components** to avoid side effects.
- **Elm:** Guarantees **no runtime errors**, making web apps more reliable.
- **Redux (JavaScript):** Enforces **immutability and pure functions**.

2. Functional Programming in Data Science and AI

- **Scala and Apache Spark:** Used for processing large datasets.
- **TensorFlow (Python):** Uses **functional graphs** for AI computations.

3. Functional Programming in Distributed Systems

- **Elixir (built on Erlang):** Supports **fault-tolerant, concurrent applications**.
- **Scala (with Akka):** Handles **real-time streaming** efficiently.

Conclusion

Modern functional programming languages provide developers with powerful tools to write **concise, maintainable, and scalable code**. While some languages, like **Haskell and Elm**, enforce **purely functional** principles, others, like **JavaScript, Python, and Kotlin**, incorporate functional features into multi-paradigm environments.

Understanding the strengths and trade-offs of each language allows developers to **choose the right tool** for their projects, whether working on **web applications, big data processing, AI, or distributed systems**. As functional programming continues to gain popularity, its principles will remain fundamental to the evolution of software development.

39 |

Chapter 2: Core Principles of Functional Programming

Pure Functions and Their Importance

Pure functions are a fundamental concept in functional programming. They serve as the building blocks for writing predictable, maintainable, and reusable code. In this section, we will explore what pure functions are, their benefits, and how they contribute to a more robust software design.

What Are Pure Functions?

A pure function is a function that satisfies two main criteria:

1. **Deterministic** – Given the same input, it will always return the same output.
2. **Side-effect free** – It does not modify any external state or variables.

Pure functions do not interact with external dependencies such as databases, files, or global variables. Instead, they take input parameters and return output solely based on those inputs.

Consider the following example of a pure function in JavaScript:

```
function add(a, b) {
    return a + b;
}

console.log(add(2, 3)); // Output: 5
console.log(add(2, 3)); // Output: 5 (always the same)
```

Here, add is a pure function because it always returns the same result for the same input, and it does not modify any external state.

In contrast, consider an impure function:

```
let total = 0;

function addToTotal(value) {
    total += value;
    return total;
}
```

```
console.log(addToTotal(5)); // Output: 5
console.log(addToTotal(5)); // Output: 10 (different result for same
input)
```

This function is **impure** because it modifies the external `total` variable, making its output dependent on external state rather than just the function arguments.

Benefits of Pure Functions

Using pure functions provides several advantages:

1. **Predictability** – Since pure functions do not depend on external state, their output is predictable, making debugging and testing easier.
2. **Reusability** – Pure functions can be reused across different parts of an application since they do not rely on any external context.
3. **Easier Testing** – Because pure functions do not depend on external variables, they are easier to test with unit tests.
4. **Concurrency-Friendly** – Since they do not modify shared state, pure functions can run in parallel without causing race conditions.
5. **Caching and Memoization** – Pure functions always return the same output for the same input, making them ideal for caching and performance optimization.

For instance, caching in functional programming can be done using **memoization**, as shown below:

```
function memoize(fn) {
    let cache = {};
    return function(...args) {
        let key = JSON.stringify(args);
        if (!cache[key]) {
            cache[key] = fn(...args);
        }
        return cache[key];
    };
}

const addMemoized = memoize(add);

console.log(addMemoized(2, 3)); // Computes and caches result: 5
console.log(addMemoized(2, 3)); // Retrieves from cache: 5
```

Since add is a pure function, memoization can be applied efficiently.

Pure Functions in Different Languages

Pure functions exist in many programming languages. Below are some examples:

Python:

```python
def add(a, b):
    return a + b

print(add(2, 3))   # Output: 5
print(add(2, 3))   # Output: 5 (always the same)
```

Haskell:

```haskell
add :: Int -> Int -> Int
add a b = a + b

main = do
    print (add 2 3)   -- Output: 5
    print (add 2 3)   -- Output: 5
```

Pure Functions and Functional Composition

Since pure functions are independent, they can be composed together to build more complex operations.

Consider function composition in JavaScript:

```javascript
const multiply = (x, y) => x * y;
const square = x => multiply(x, x);

console.log(square(4)); // Output: 16
console.log(square(5)); // Output: 25
```

Function composition allows us to combine multiple pure functions to create a pipeline of transformations.

A more advanced example using **composition**:

```
const compose = (...functions) => (value) =>
    functions.reduceRight((acc, fn) => fn(acc), value);

const addOne = x => x + 1;
const double = x => x * 2;

const addOneThenDouble = compose(double, addOne);

console.log(addOneThenDouble(3)); // Output: 8
```

Here, `addOneThenDouble(3)` first adds 1 (resulting in 4) and then doubles it (resulting in 8).

Avoiding Side Effects

To ensure that functions remain pure, it is essential to **avoid side effects**. Side effects occur when a function:

- Modifies a global or external variable
- Writes to a database or file
- Logs to the console
- Sends an HTTP request
- Reads user input

For example, the function below introduces a side effect:

```
function logAndAdd(a, b) {
    console.log(`Adding ${a} and ${b}`);
    return a + b;
}
```

Although this function returns a sum, it also logs to the console, making it **impure**.

A better approach would be:

```
function add(a, b) {
    return a + b;
}
```

```
// Logging is done outside the function
console.log(add(3, 4));
```

By separating concerns, we maintain purity while still achieving the necessary functionality.

Real-World Use Cases

Pure functions are widely used in various applications, including:

1. **Functional UI Development** – Libraries like **React** rely on pure functions (components) for rendering.
2. **Data Processing Pipelines** – Functions like map, reduce, and filter in JavaScript allow for clean, functional data transformations.
3. **Mathematical Computations** – Pure functions are perfect for algorithms and mathematical calculations.

Consider a **functional approach** to filtering data:

```
const users = [
    { name: "Alice", age: 25 },
    { name: "Bob", age: 30 },
    { name: "Charlie", age: 35 }
];

const isOver30 = user => user.age > 30;
const usersOver30 = users.filter(isOver30);

console.log(usersOver30);
// Output: [{ name: "Charlie", age: 35 }]
```

Conclusion

Pure functions are a cornerstone of functional programming. They provide **predictability**, **reusability**, **easier testing**, and **better performance** by avoiding side effects. Writing pure functions encourages a **declarative** programming style, leading to cleaner and more maintainable code.

By embracing **pure functions**, developers can build more scalable and resilient software systems. The next section will explore **immutability**, another crucial principle of functional programming.

Immutability and Its Role in Software Design

Immutability is one of the core principles of functional programming. It ensures that data cannot be modified after it has been created, leading to more predictable and reliable code. In this section, we will explore what immutability means, why it is important, how it is implemented in different programming languages, and how it impacts software design.

What Is Immutability?

Immutability refers to the idea that once a value has been assigned to a variable or data structure, it cannot be changed. Instead of modifying existing data, new values are created whenever changes are required.

For example, in JavaScript, primitive values like numbers and strings are inherently immutable:

```
let x = 5;
x = x + 1; // This does not change the value of 5, but reassigns x to
a new value
```

Here, 5 remains unchanged, and a new value 6 is assigned to x. However, objects and arrays in JavaScript are mutable by default:

```
let arr = [1, 2, 3];
arr.push(4); // Mutates the original array
```

To enforce immutability, we use functional techniques such as copying and returning new structures instead of modifying existing ones:

```
let arr = [1, 2, 3];
let newArr = [...arr, 4]; // Creates a new array instead of modifying
the original

console.log(arr);      // Output: [1, 2, 3]
console.log(newArr);   // Output: [1, 2, 3, 4]
```

Why Is Immutability Important?

Immutability brings several benefits that make software development more manageable and scalable.

1. Predictability and Debugging

Mutable state leads to unpredictable behavior because multiple parts of an application can modify the same data, causing unexpected side effects. With immutability, data does not change once it is set, making it easier to reason about program behavior.

Consider a scenario where a function modifies a global variable:

```
let counter = 0;

function increment() {
    counter++; // Mutates global state
}

increment();
console.log(counter); // Output: 1

increment();
console.log(counter); // Output: 2 (unexpected changes)
```

Here, the function `increment` changes a variable outside its scope, leading to implicit dependencies. A more predictable approach is to return a new value instead:

```
function increment(count) {
    return count + 1; // Returns a new value instead of modifying
state
}

let counter = 0;
counter = increment(counter);
console.log(counter); // Output: 1

counter = increment(counter);
console.log(counter); // Output: 2
```

This makes the function self-contained and predictable.

2. Concurrency and Multi-Threading

In multi-threaded applications, mutable state can lead to race conditions where multiple threads try to modify the same variable at the same time. Since immutable data cannot be changed, it eliminates these issues and makes concurrent programming safer.

For example, in JavaScript, objects can be mutated by different parts of the application:

```javascript
let user = { name: "Alice", age: 25 };

function updateAge(obj, newAge) {
    obj.age = newAge; // Mutates the original object
}

updateAge(user, 30);
console.log(user); // Output: { name: "Alice", age: 30 }
```

Instead, an immutable approach ensures that updates do not affect the original object:

```javascript
function updateAge(obj, newAge) {
    return { ...obj, age: newAge }; // Returns a new object instead
of mutating
}

let user = { name: "Alice", age: 25 };
let updatedUser = updateAge(user, 30);

console.log(user);        // Output: { name: "Alice", age: 25 }
console.log(updatedUser); // Output: { name: "Alice", age: 30 }
```

By avoiding shared state mutations, concurrency issues are minimized.

3. Functional Programming and State Management

Immutability is at the core of state management in functional programming. Libraries like Redux in JavaScript enforce immutability to ensure that application state remains predictable.

A Redux reducer follows the principle of immutability:

```javascript
function counterReducer(state = { count: 0 }, action) {
    switch (action.type) {
        case "INCREMENT":
            return { ...state, count: state.count + 1 }; // Returns a
new state object
        case "DECREMENT":
            return { ...state, count: state.count - 1 };
```

```
        default:
            return state;
    }
}
```

Here, the reducer does not mutate `state` but instead returns a new state object, ensuring predictable updates.

How Immutability Is Enforced in Different Languages

Different programming languages provide mechanisms to enforce immutability.

1. JavaScript and TypeScript

JavaScript provides `const` to prevent reassignment but does not make objects truly immutable. The `Object.freeze` method prevents modification:

```
const obj = Object.freeze({ name: "Alice" });
obj.name = "Bob"; // Error in strict mode
console.log(obj.name); // Output: Alice
```

However, `Object.freeze` is shallow, meaning nested objects are still mutable.

2. Python

Python supports immutable data structures like tuples:

```
my_tuple = (1, 2, 3)
# my_tuple[0] = 4  # Error: Tuples are immutable
```

Python also has the `dataclasses` module with `frozen=True` to enforce immutability:

```
from dataclasses import dataclass

@dataclass(frozen=True)
class Person:
    name: str
    age: int
```

```
p = Person("Alice", 25)
# p.age = 30  # Error: Cannot modify frozen dataclass
```

3. Scala

Scala embraces immutability by default. Variables declared with `val` cannot be reassigned:

```
val x = 10
// x = 20  // Error: reassignment to val
```

Scala collections like `List` are immutable:

```
val nums = List(1, 2, 3)
val newNums = nums :+ 4  // Creates a new list
println(nums)      // Output: List(1, 2, 3)
println(newNums)   // Output: List(1, 2, 3, 4)
```

4. Haskell

Haskell enforces immutability by default, making it a pure functional language:

```
add x y = x + y   -- Cannot modify x or y
```

Haskell's data structures are immutable, ensuring safety in concurrent applications.

Trade-offs of Immutability

While immutability provides numerous benefits, it also comes with trade-offs:

1. **Increased Memory Usage** – Since new copies of data structures are created instead of modifying existing ones, more memory may be used.
2. **Performance Overhead** – Copying large data structures can be expensive, but persistent data structures mitigate this issue.
3. **Learning Curve** – Developers used to imperative programming may find immutability restrictive at first.

Despite these trade-offs, immutability is a powerful concept that leads to better software design.

Conclusion

Immutability is a crucial principle in functional programming, providing **predictability, safety, and reliability** in software development. By preventing unwanted state mutations, immutability makes debugging easier, improves concurrency handling, and enhances state management in applications.

Embracing immutability requires a shift in mindset, but its benefits far outweigh its challenges. The next section will explore **higher-order functions**, another fundamental concept in functional programming.

Recursion vs. Iteration in Functional Programming

Recursion is a fundamental concept in functional programming, allowing functions to call themselves to solve problems. It serves as an alternative to iteration, commonly used in imperative programming. This section explores the differences between recursion and iteration, the advantages of recursion in functional programming, tail call optimization, and practical use cases of recursion.

Understanding Recursion

Recursion occurs when a function calls itself within its own definition. A recursive function consists of two main parts:

1. **Base Case** – A condition that stops the recursion.
2. **Recursive Case** – A call to the function itself with a smaller input.

Here is a simple example of recursion in JavaScript:

```
function countdown(n) {
    if (n <= 0) {
        console.log("Done!");
        return;
    }
    console.log(n);
    countdown(n - 1); // Recursive call with a smaller input
}

countdown(5);
```

```
3
2
1
Done!
```

The function continues calling itself with a decreasing value of n until it reaches the base case
(n <= 0), at which point recursion stops.

Recursion vs. Iteration

Iteration and recursion both solve problems through repeated steps. However, they differ in
implementation and how they handle state.

1. Iteration Approach

In imperative programming, loops (such as for or while) are used to achieve repetition.

Example: Factorial using iteration

```javascript
function factorial(n) {
    let result = 1;
    for (let i = 2; i <= n; i++) {
        result *= i;
    }
    return result;
}

console.log(factorial(5)); // Output: 120
```

2. Recursive Approach

Functional programming favors recursion over iteration, avoiding mutable variables.

Example: Factorial using recursion

```javascript
function factorial(n) {
    if (n === 0) return 1; // Base case
    return n * factorial(n - 1); // Recursive case
}
```

```
console.log(factorial(5)); // Output: 120
```

Both approaches produce the same result, but recursion avoids explicit loops and variable mutation.

Advantages of Recursion in Functional Programming

Recursion is preferred in functional programming for several reasons:

1. **Immutability** – Since recursion does not rely on mutable state (like loop counters), it fits naturally with functional programming.
2. **Declarative Approach** – Recursive functions express logic more clearly, focusing on the **what** rather than the **how**.
3. **Better for Tree and Graph Traversal** – Recursive functions simplify operations on hierarchical structures like trees.
4. **Enables Functional Composition** – Recursion allows chaining of function calls, making composition easier.

For example, recursively computing the sum of an array:

```
function sum(arr) {
    if (arr.length === 0) return 0; // Base case
    return arr[0] + sum(arr.slice(1)); // Recursive case
}

console.log(sum([1, 2, 3, 4, 5])); // Output: 15
```

Here, the first element is added to the sum of the remaining elements, breaking the problem into smaller subproblems.

Tail Recursion and Optimization

One common issue with recursion is **stack overflow** due to excessive function calls. Consider the following recursive function:

```
function sum(n) {
    if (n === 0) return 0;
    return n + sum(n - 1);
}
```

```
console.log(sum(100000)); // Stack overflow error
```

Each recursive call adds a new frame to the call stack, causing memory overhead.

Tail Call Optimization

Some languages optimize recursion using **tail call optimization (TCO)**. A tail-recursive function is a function where the recursive call is the **last** operation before returning.

Example of a tail-recursive function:

```
function sumTail(n, acc = 0) {
    if (n === 0) return acc;
    return sumTail(n - 1, acc + n); // Tail call: no additional
computation after recursive call
}

console.log(sumTail(100000)); // No stack overflow with TCO-supported
engines
```

In tail recursion, the previous stack frame is **not needed**, reducing memory consumption.

Languages like Haskell and Scala support TCO by default, while JavaScript (as of ES6) provides it only in optimized environments.

Practical Use Cases of Recursion

Recursion is commonly used in various applications, including:

1. Traversing Trees and Graphs

Recursive functions make traversing hierarchical structures intuitive.

Example: Recursive tree traversal

```
const tree = {
    value: 1,
    children: [
        { value: 2, children: [{ value: 4, children: [] }, { value:
5, children: [] }] },
```

```
        { value: 3, children: [{ value: 6, children: [] }, { value:
7, children: [] }] }
    ]
};

function traverse(node) {
    console.log(node.value);
    node.children.forEach(traverse);
}

traverse(tree);
```

This function prints each node's value recursively.

2. Fibonacci Sequence

The Fibonacci sequence can be implemented recursively:

```
function fibonacci(n) {
    if (n <= 1) return n; // Base cases
    return fibonacci(n - 1) + fibonacci(n - 2); // Recursive case
}

console.log(fibonacci(5)); // Output: 5
```

However, this naive implementation is inefficient due to duplicate computations.

Optimized version using memoization:

```
function fibonacciMemo(n, memo = {}) {
    if (n in memo) return memo[n];
    if (n <= 1) return n;
    memo[n] = fibonacciMemo(n - 1, memo) + fibonacciMemo(n - 2, memo);
    return memo[n];
}

console.log(fibonacciMemo(50)); // Fast execution
```

Memoization stores computed values, improving efficiency.

3. Sorting Algorithms

Many sorting algorithms rely on recursion, such as **merge sort** and **quick sort**.

Example: Quick Sort

```
function quickSort(arr) {
    if (arr.length <= 1) return arr; // Base case
    let pivot = arr[arr.length - 1];
    let left = arr.filter(x => x < pivot);
    let right = arr.filter(x => x > pivot);
    return [...quickSort(left), pivot, ...quickSort(right)];
}

console.log(quickSort([3, 1, 4, 1, 5, 9, 2, 6])); // Sorted array
```

Quick sort recursively partitions the array into smaller subsets, sorting them efficiently.

When to Use Recursion vs. Iteration

While recursion is powerful, it is not always the best choice. Consider the following:

Factor	Recursion	Iteration
Performance	Can be slow due to stack usage	Generally faster due to fewer function calls
Memory Usage	Can cause stack overflow	Uses constant memory ($O(1)$)
Readability	Clearer for tree/graph traversal	Simpler for loops and repetitive tasks
Tail Call Support	Some languages optimize recursion	No need for special optimization

For problems like **looping over numbers** or **accumulating values**, iteration is preferable. For **hierarchical data processing**, recursion provides a more natural solution.

Conclusion

Recursion is a fundamental concept in functional programming, offering a declarative way to handle problems. While it can lead to stack overflow, techniques like tail call optimization and memoization mitigate performance concerns. Recursion is particularly useful for **tree traversal, sorting, and solving complex mathematical problems**.

By understanding when to use recursion over iteration, developers can write **more expressive and maintainable code**, taking full advantage of functional programming principles.

The next section will explore **lazy evaluation**, another powerful technique in functional programming.

Lazy Evaluation and Its Benefits

Lazy evaluation is a powerful concept in functional programming that delays the computation of an expression until its value is actually needed. This technique allows programs to be more efficient, reducing unnecessary computations and improving performance. In this section, we will explore the principles of lazy evaluation, its benefits, implementation across different programming languages, and real-world applications.

Understanding Lazy Evaluation

Lazy evaluation is a strategy where expressions are not evaluated immediately but only when required. This contrasts with **eager evaluation**, which computes values as soon as they are encountered.

Example of Eager vs. Lazy Evaluation

Consider an eager evaluation approach in JavaScript:

```
function eagerMultiply(a, b) {
    return a * b;
}

console.log(eagerMultiply(5, 10)); // Output: 50 (computed
immediately)
```

In contrast, a lazy evaluation approach defers computation:

```
function lazyMultiply(a, b) {
    return () => a * b; // Returns a function that computes the value
when called
}
```

```
const result = lazyMultiply(5, 10); // No computation yet
console.log(result()); // Output: 50 (computed when needed)
```

With lazy evaluation, the multiplication is delayed until explicitly invoked.

Benefits of Lazy Evaluation

Lazy evaluation offers several advantages:

1. **Performance Optimization**
   - Avoids unnecessary computations.
   - Improves efficiency in scenarios where only part of a data structure is needed.
2. **Infinite Data Structures**
   - Enables handling of theoretically infinite sequences without consuming excessive memory.
3. **Improved Modularity**
   - Supports function chaining and composition without intermediate results.
4. **Better Memory Management**
   - Prevents unnecessary memory allocation by computing values only when required.

Lazy Evaluation in Functional Programming Languages

Functional programming languages often provide built-in support for lazy evaluation. Let's examine how it works in different languages.

Lazy Evaluation in Haskell

Haskell is a purely functional language where lazy evaluation is the default. Consider the following example:

```
ones :: [Int]
ones = 1 : ones   -- Creates an infinite list of ones

take 5 ones   -- Output: [1,1,1,1,1]
```

Although ones is an infinite list, Haskell only evaluates the first five elements due to lazy evaluation.

Lazy Evaluation in JavaScript

JavaScript does not have built-in lazy evaluation but can implement it using **generators**.

Example: Infinite sequence using generators:

```
function* naturalNumbers() {
    let n = 1;
    while (true) {
        yield n++;
    }
}
```

```
const numbers = naturalNumbers();
console.log(numbers.next().value); // Output: 1
console.log(numbers.next().value); // Output: 2
console.log(numbers.next().value); // Output: 3
```

The generator function `naturalNumbers` produces numbers lazily, generating the next value only when requested.

Lazy Evaluation in Data Structures

Lazy evaluation is particularly useful for optimizing data structure operations.

Lazy Loading in Lists

In eager evaluation, filtering a list requires computing all elements upfront:

```
const numbers = [1, 2, 3, 4, 5, 6];
const evens = numbers.filter(n => n % 2 === 0);

console.log(evens); // Output: [2, 4, 6]
```

With lazy evaluation, filtering is deferred:

```
function* lazyFilter(arr, predicate) {
    for (let item of arr) {
        if (predicate(item)) yield item;
    }
}
```

```
const lazyEvens = lazyFilter(numbers, n => n % 2 === 0);
console.log([...lazyEvens]); // Output: [2, 4, 6]
```

Here, elements are checked **only when needed**, improving efficiency.

Stream Processing

Lazy evaluation is commonly used in **stream processing**, where large datasets are processed in chunks.

Example: Processing log files lazily:

```
const fs = require('fs');
const readline = require('readline');

async function processLogFile(filePath) {
    const fileStream = fs.createReadStream(filePath);
    const rl = readline.createInterface({ input: fileStream });

    for await (const line of rl) {
        if (line.includes('ERROR')) console.log(line); // Only
processes necessary lines
    }
}

processLogFile('logs.txt');
```

Here, the log file is read **line by line** instead of loading the entire file into memory.

Comparison of Lazy and Eager Evaluation

The following table compares lazy and eager evaluation:

Feature	Lazy Evaluation	Eager Evaluation
Execution Timing	Delays computation until needed	Computes immediately

Performance	Optimized, avoids unnecessary work	Can be inefficient
Memory Usage	Efficient for large data sets	May consume more memory
Suitability	Best for infinite sequences, streams	Best for simple, immediate calculations

Real-World Applications of Lazy Evaluation

Lazy evaluation has many practical applications in software development.

1. Functional Programming Libraries

Libraries such as **Lodash** and **Ramda** implement lazy evaluation for data processing.

Example: Using Lodash's lazy evaluation:

```
const _ = require('lodash');

const numbers = _.range(1, 1000000); // Large dataset
const result = _(numbers)
    .filter(n => n % 2 === 0)
    .map(n => n * 2)
    .take(10)
    .value(); // Execution happens here

console.log(result); // Output: [4, 8, 12, 16, 20, 24, 28, 32, 36, 40]
```

Here, the operations are **chained but not executed** until .value() is called.

2. Database Query Optimization

Databases use lazy evaluation when executing SQL queries. Instead of fetching all records immediately, results are retrieved **on demand**.

Example: SQL query with lazy execution:

```
SELECT * FROM users WHERE age > 30 LIMIT 10;
```

The database does **not** fetch all users over 30; it stops once **10 results** are retrieved.

3. Web Development and Rendering

React uses lazy evaluation to improve rendering performance. Components are only rendered when needed.

Example: React's `lazy` function:

```
import React, { Suspense, lazy } from 'react';

const LazyComponent = lazy(() => import('./HeavyComponent'));

function App() {
    return (
        <Suspense fallback={<div>Loading...</div>}>
            <LazyComponent />
        </Suspense>
    );
}
```

Here, `HeavyComponent` is **only loaded when required**, improving performance.

When to Use Lazy Evaluation

Lazy evaluation is beneficial in many scenarios:

- **Processing large datasets** (e.g., logs, databases)
- **Working with infinite sequences** (e.g., number generators)
- **Optimizing memory usage** in constrained environments
- **Enhancing performance in functional pipelines**

However, it **should not be used indiscriminately**. If all values are needed immediately, eager evaluation may be more efficient.

Conclusion

Lazy evaluation is a fundamental concept in functional programming that **delays computations** until necessary. It provides **performance optimizations, supports infinite data structures, improves modularity, and optimizes memory usage**.

By leveraging lazy evaluation, developers can **write more efficient, scalable applications**, especially in **data processing, functional pipelines, and UI rendering**.

The next section will explore **pattern matching and destructuring**, another essential concept in functional programming.

Referential Transparency and Predictable Computations

Referential transparency is a key principle in functional programming that ensures expressions can be replaced with their values without changing program behavior. This property enhances code readability, testability, and maintainability while enabling powerful optimizations. In this section, we will explore referential transparency, its advantages, examples in different programming languages, and its role in functional programming.

Understanding Referential Transparency

A function or expression is **referentially transparent** if it can be replaced with its computed value **without affecting the program's behavior**. This means the function produces the same output given the same input, with no side effects.

Example of Referential Transparency

Consider a simple mathematical function:

```
function add(a, b) {

    return a + b;

}
```

```
console.log(add(2, 3)); // Output: 5
```

Since add(2, 3) always returns 5, it can be replaced with 5 anywhere in the program without changing the logic.

In contrast, a function with side effects **violates referential transparency**:

```
let total = 0;
```

```
function addToTotal(value) {

    total += value;

    return total;

}
```

```
console.log(addToTotal(5)); // Output: 5
```

```
console.log(addToTotal(5)); // Output: 10 (different output for same
input)
```

Since `addToTotal(5)` does not always return the same value, it is **not referentially transparent**.

Why Referential Transparency Matters

Referential transparency provides several advantages in functional programming:

1. **Predictability**
   o Ensures that functions behave consistently without hidden dependencies.
2. **Simplified Debugging**
   o Since functions do not depend on external state, debugging becomes easier.
3. **Memoization and Optimization**
   o Since function calls always return the same output, caching results improves performance.
4. **Parallelism and Concurrency**
   o Programs can be safely executed in parallel without race conditions.
5. **Mathematical Reasoning**
   o Allows programs to be understood and reasoned about using algebraic transformations.

Examples of Referential Transparency

Example 1: Pure Functions in JavaScript

Referential transparency is closely linked to **pure functions**.

Pure function (referentially transparent):

```
function square(x) {

    return x * x;

}
```

```
console.log(square(4)); // Output: 16

console.log(square(4)); // Output: 16 (always the same)
```

Since `square(4)` always evaluates to `16`, it can be replaced with `16` anywhere in the program.

Impure function (not referentially transparent):

```
let factor = 2;
```

```
function multiply(x) {

    return x * factor;

}
```

```
console.log(multiply(3)); // Output depends on `factor`

factor = 5;

console.log(multiply(3)); // Output changes (not predictable)
```

Here, `multiply(3)` produces different results depending on `factor`, violating referential transparency.

Example 2: Referential Transparency in Haskell

Haskell enforces referential transparency by design:

```
square x = x * x
```

```
main = print (square 4) -- Always outputs 16
```

Since Haskell functions cannot have side effects, `square(4)` is **guaranteed** to return 16 every time.

Example 3: Side Effects Breaking Referential Transparency

Functions interacting with external systems (e.g., databases, files) are **not referentially transparent**.

```
function getRandomNumber() {

    return Math.random(); // Produces a different value each time

}
```

```
console.log(getRandomNumber()); // Output changes on every call
```

Since `getRandomNumber()` does not return the same result consistently, it **violates** referential transparency.

Memoization and Optimization

Referential transparency allows **memoization**, a technique for storing function results to avoid redundant computations.

Example: Caching function results:

```
function memoize(fn) {
```

```
    let cache = {};

    return function (...args) {

        let key = JSON.stringify(args);

        if (!cache[key]) {

            cache[key] = fn(...args);

        }

        return cache[key];

    };

}


const squareMemoized = memoize(square);


console.log(squareMemoized(5)); // Computes and caches result: 25

console.log(squareMemoized(5)); // Retrieves from cache: 25
```

Since `square(5)` is referentially transparent, **memoization is effective**.

Functional Composition and Referential Transparency

Functional programming encourages **function composition**, where functions are combined to form larger expressions.

Example: Composing functions in JavaScript:

```
const double = x => x * 2;

const increment = x => x + 1;
```

```
const doubleThenIncrement = x => increment(double(x));
```

```
console.log(doubleThenIncrement(3)); // Output: 7
```

Since both `double` and `increment` are referentially transparent, the entire composition remains predictable.

Impact on Parallelism and Concurrency

Referential transparency enables safe **parallel execution**. Since functions do not depend on shared state, they can run concurrently without conflicts.

Example: Processing an array in parallel:

```
const numbers = [1, 2, 3, 4, 5];
```

```
const squaredNumbers = numbers.map(square);
```

```
console.log(squaredNumbers); // Output: [1, 4, 9, 16, 25]
```

Each function call is independent, allowing **safe parallel execution**.

In contrast, a function modifying a shared variable **is not parallel-safe**:

```
let sum = 0;
```

```
numbers.forEach(num => {
    sum += num * num; // Side effect: modifies `sum`
});
```

```
console.log(sum); // Output depends on execution order
```

Here, the result **depends on execution order**, making it unsafe for parallel processing.

Real-World Applications of Referential Transparency

1. **Functional UI Development**
   - Libraries like **React** encourage referential transparency by using **pure components**.

javascript

```
function Button({ label }) {

    return <button>{label}</button>; // Always produces the same
output

}
```

2.
3. **Database Query Optimization**
   - SQL queries that do not modify data are referentially transparent.

sql

```
SELECT * FROM users WHERE age > 30;
```

4. This query **always returns the same results** for the same database state.
5. **Compiler Optimizations**
   - Compilers optimize referentially transparent functions by replacing expressions with computed values.
6. **Caching in Web Development**
   - APIs returning consistent results can be cached effectively.

javascript

```
fetch('https://api.example.com/data')

    .then(response => response.json())

    .then(data => console.log(data));
```

7. If the API result is predictable, caching improves performance.

Challenges and Limitations

While referential transparency has many benefits, it also has limitations:

Challenge	Description
Handling Side Effects	Functions interacting with external systems (e.g., I/O, databases) break referential transparency.
Performance Overhead	Some computations (e.g., large data processing) may be inefficient without mutation.
State Management Complexity	Managing application state without modifying global variables can be challenging.

Functional programming addresses these challenges using **monads**, **immutability**, and **pure functions**.

Conclusion

Referential transparency is a **core principle** of functional programming that ensures **predictable computations, easier debugging, efficient caching, and safer parallel execution**. By avoiding side effects and ensuring that functions return consistent outputs, functional programming promotes **more maintainable and scalable software**.

The next section will explore **higher-order functions**, another fundamental concept in functional programming.

Chapter 3: Functional Programming Techniques

Function Composition and Chaining

Function composition is a fundamental concept in functional programming that allows developers to build complex operations by combining simpler functions. This technique improves code readability, maintainability, and reusability by breaking down logic into smaller, composable units.

Understanding Function Composition

$$(f \circ g)(x) = f(g(x))$$

This means that g is applied to x, and then f is applied to the result of $g(x)$. In programming, function composition enables building complex functionality from simpler, reusable functions.

Consider a simple example in JavaScript:

```
const toUpperCase = str => str.toUpperCase();

const exclaim = str => str + "!";

const repeat = str => str.repeat(2);



const compose = (f, g) => x => f(g(x));



const shout = compose(toUpperCase, exclaim);

console.log(shout("hello")); // "HELLO!"
```

Here, `compose` is a higher-order function that takes two functions, f and g, and returns a new function that applies g to its input and then applies f to the result.

Function Chaining vs. Composition

Function chaining is closely related to function composition but differs in implementation. Chaining is often associated with object-oriented and fluent-style APIs, where methods are called sequentially on an object.

Consider the following example using JavaScript's built-in array methods:

```
const numbers = [1, 2, 3, 4, 5];

const result = numbers
  .map(x => x * 2)
  .filter(x => x > 5)
  .reduce((sum, x) => sum + x, 0);

console.log(result); // 18
```

Here, `map`, `filter`, and `reduce` are chained together, making the code more readable and declarative.

In contrast, function composition uses nested calls:

```
const double = x => x * 2;
const greaterThanFive = x => x > 5;
const sum = (acc, x) => acc + x;

const processNumbers = numbers =>
  numbers.map(double).filter(greaterThanFive).reduce(sum, 0);
```

```
console.log(processNumbers([1, 2, 3, 4, 5])); // 18
```

Both approaches are valid, but function composition is preferred in functional programming due to its declarative nature and ease of refactoring.

Composing Multiple Functions

When composing more than two functions, a utility function like compose can be extended to support multiple functions:

```
const compose = (...funcs) => x => funcs.reduceRight((acc, fn) =>
fn(acc), x);
```

```
const shoutLoudly = compose(repeat, exclaim, toUpperCase);

console.log(shoutLoudly("hello")); // "HELLO!HELLO!"
```

The compose function takes any number of functions and applies them from right to left, ensuring the output of one function becomes the input of the next.

Function Composition in Different Languages

While JavaScript provides flexibility for composing functions, many functional programming languages have built-in support for composition.

Haskell

In Haskell, function composition is built into the language using the (.) operator:

```
toUpperCase :: String -> String

toUpperCase = map toUpper
```

```
exclaim :: String -> String

exclaim str = str ++ "!"
```

```
shout :: String -> String

shout = toUpperCase . exclaim


main = putStrLn (shout "hello") -- "HELLO!"
```

Here, `toUpperCase . exclaim` creates a new function by composing `toUpperCase` and `exclaim`.

Python

Python's `functools.reduce` can help with function composition:

```
from functools import reduce


def to_uppercase(s): return s.upper()

def exclaim(s): return s + "!"

def repeat(s): return s * 2


def compose(*funcs):

    return lambda x: reduce(lambda acc, f: f(acc), reversed(funcs), x)


shout_loudly = compose(to_uppercase, exclaim, repeat)

print(shout_loudly("hello"))  # "HELLO!HELLO!"
```

Practical Use Cases

Data Transformation Pipelines

Function composition is widely used in data transformation pipelines where multiple transformations are applied sequentially:

```
const processUserData = compose(

  JSON.stringify,

  data => ({ ...data, active: true }),

  user => ({ id: user.id, name: user.name })

);



const user = { id: 1, name: "Alice", email: "alice@example.com" };

console.log(processUserData(user));

// '{"id":1,"name":"Alice","active":true}'
```

Middleware in Web Frameworks

In frameworks like Express.js, function composition is used in middleware processing:

```
const logger = (req, res, next) => { console.log(req.url); next(); };

const auth = (req, res, next) => { if (!req.user)
res.status(401).end(); else next(); };



const app = require('express')();

app.use(logger, auth);
```

Here, middleware functions are composed and executed sequentially.

Functional Reactive Programming (FRP)

Functional composition is also a core concept in reactive programming libraries like RxJS:

```
import { fromEvent } from "rxjs";

import { map, filter } from "rxjs/operators";


const keypresses = fromEvent(document, 'keydown').pipe(

  map(event => event.key),

  filter(key => key === 'Enter')

);


keypresses.subscribe(key => console.log(`You pressed: ${key}`));
```

Benefits of Function Composition

1. **Modularity** – Encourages writing small, reusable functions.
2. **Readability** – Expresses logic declaratively, reducing cognitive load.
3. **Testability** – Functions can be unit-tested in isolation.
4. **Maintainability** – Easier to refactor and extend without breaking existing code.
5. **Avoids Side Effects** – Encourages pure function usage, minimizing unintended behavior.

Conclusion

Function composition and chaining are powerful techniques in functional programming that enable developers to create scalable, maintainable, and reusable code. By leveraging these patterns, developers can structure applications in a way that aligns with the principles of functional programming, leading to more predictable and robust software.

Currying and Partial Application

Currying and partial application are two fundamental techniques in functional programming that enhance code modularity, reusability, and readability. These techniques allow functions to be transformed into more flexible and composable units, making them easier to work with in a functional programming paradigm.

Understanding Currying

Currying is a technique where a function with multiple arguments is transformed into a sequence of functions, each taking a single argument. This means instead of passing all arguments at once, we pass them one at a time, returning a new function at each step until all arguments have been provided.

Mathematical Representation of Currying

In mathematical notation, a function $f(x, y, z)$ can be curried into:

```
f: (x, y, z) → result

f: x → (y → (z → result))
```

Each function takes one argument and returns a new function until all arguments are consumed.

Currying in JavaScript

In JavaScript, functions can be curried manually or using utility functions. Here's an example of manually currying a function:

```
const add = x => y => z => x + y + z;



console.log(add(2)(3)(4)); // 9
```

The add function takes one argument at a time and returns a new function until all three arguments have been provided.

We can also implement a general currying function:

```
const curry = (fn) =>

  (...args) =>

    args.length >= fn.length

      ? fn(...args)
```

```
    : curry(fn.bind(null, ...args));


const multiply = (a, b, c) => a * b * c;

const curriedMultiply = curry(multiply);


console.log(curriedMultiply(2)(3)(4)); // 24

console.log(curriedMultiply(2, 3)(4)); // 24

console.log(curriedMultiply(2)(3, 4)); // 24
```

This curry function dynamically curies any function, allowing arguments to be applied incrementally.

Currying in Python

In Python, currying can be achieved using function closures or functools.partial:

```
def curry_add(x):

    def add_y(y):

        def add_z(z):

            return x + y + z

        return add_z

    return add_y


add_curried = curry_add(2)(3)(4)

print(add_curried)  # 9
```

Alternatively, using functools.partial:

```python
from functools import partial

def multiply(x, y, z):
    return x * y * z

curried_multiply = partial(multiply, 2)
print(curried_multiply(3, 4))   # 24
```

Benefits of Currying

1. **Modularity** – Functions become more composable and reusable.
2. **Function Reusability** – Partial applications can be derived from curried functions.
3. **Avoids Repetition** – Useful when the same argument is used multiple times.
4. **Enhances Readability** – Expresses functions in a declarative manner.
5. **Functional Composition** – Works seamlessly with function composition techniques.

Partial Application

Partial application is similar to currying but differs in that it allows applying some arguments to a function while keeping it callable for remaining arguments. This creates a new function with pre-filled parameters.

Partial Application in JavaScript

Using JavaScript's bind method:

```javascript
const multiply = (a, b, c) => a * b * c;
const multiplyByTwo = multiply.bind(null, 2);


console.log(multiplyByTwo(3, 4)); // 24
```

This pre-fills the first argument (2), creating a new function that only requires the remaining arguments.

Alternatively, using a custom function:

```
const   partial   =   (fn,   ...presetArgs)   =>   (...laterArgs)   =>
fn(...presetArgs,  ...laterArgs);
```

```
const add = (a, b, c) => a + b + c;
```

```
const addFive = partial(add, 5);
```

```
console.log(addFive(3, 2)); // 10
```

Partial Application in Python

Python's `functools.partial` provides built-in support for partial application:

```
from functools import partial
```

```
def power(base, exponent):
    return base ** exponent
```

```
square = partial(power, exponent=2)
```

```
cube = partial(power, exponent=3)
```

```
print(square(4))  # 16
```

```
print(cube(2))    # 8
```

Here, `square` and `cube` are specialized versions of `power`, pre-filling the exponent argument.

Currying vs. Partial Application

Feature	Currying	Partial Application
Argument Handling	Breaks function into unary functions	Pre-fills some arguments
Flexibility	Requires calling in sequence	Allows providing arguments out of order
Readability	Improves function composition	Reduces code duplication

Real-World Applications of Currying and Partial Application

Event Handling in JavaScript

Currying is useful in event handling where multiple handlers share common parameters:

```
const handleEvent = type => element => callback =>
  element.addEventListener(type, callback);


const clickHandler = handleEvent("click");


clickHandler(document.getElementById("button"))(()                    =>
alert("Clicked!"));
```

Functional Middleware in Express.js

Partial application simplifies middleware creation:

```
const authenticate = role => (req, res, next) => {

  if (req.user && req.user.role === role) next();

  else res.status(403).send("Forbidden");

};
```

```
app.get("/admin",    authenticate("admin"),    (req,    res)    =>
res.send("Welcome Admin"));
```

Data Processing Pipelines

Currying is widely used in data processing:

```
const filterBy = key => value => array => array.filter(item =>
item[key] === value);
```

```
const filterByRole = filterBy("role")("admin");
```

```
const users = [

  { name: "Alice", role: "admin" },

  { name: "Bob", role: "user" }

];
```

```
console.log(filterByRole(users)); // [{ name: "Alice", role: "admin"
}]
```

Configuration Management

Partial application simplifies configurations:

```
def configure_app(env, debug, db_url):

    return f"Configuring {env} - Debug: {debug}, DB: {db_url}"


dev_config = partial(configure_app, "development", True)

prod_config = partial(configure_app, "production", False)


print(dev_config("sqlite://dev.db"))    # Configuring development -
Debug: True, DB: sqlite://dev.db
```

Conclusion

Currying and partial application are essential techniques in functional programming that enhance modularity, function reusability, and code readability. These concepts allow developers to create flexible and maintainable codebases by enabling functions to be applied incrementally. By mastering these techniques, programmers can write cleaner, more expressive, and scalable functional code.

Recursion vs. Iteration in Functional Programming

Recursion and iteration are two fundamental techniques for solving problems that involve repetitive computations. While iteration is more common in imperative programming, recursion plays a significant role in functional programming. Understanding the differences between these two approaches, their advantages, and their limitations is crucial for writing efficient functional code.

Understanding Recursion

Recursion is a technique where a function calls itself to solve a smaller instance of the same problem. This continues until a base case is reached, which stops the recursive calls.

Basic Structure of Recursion

A recursive function typically consists of:

1. **Base Case** – The stopping condition that prevents infinite recursion.
2. **Recursive Case** – The function calls itself with a smaller problem.

Example: A simple recursive function to calculate the factorial of a number:

```
const factorial = (n) => {

  if (n === 0) return 1;   // Base case

  return n * factorial(n - 1);   // Recursive case

};


console.log(factorial(5)); // 120
```

Here, `factorial(5)` calls `factorial(4)`, which calls `factorial(3)`, and so on, until the base case `n === 0` is reached.

Recursion in Different Languages

Python Example

```python
def factorial(n):

    if n == 0:

        return 1

    return n * factorial(n - 1)


print(factorial(5))  # 120
```

Haskell Example

Haskell, being a purely functional language, heavily relies on recursion:

```haskell
factorial :: Integer -> Integer

factorial 0 = 1
```

```
factorial n = n * factorial (n - 1)



main = print (factorial 5)   -- 120
```

Types of Recursion

1. **Direct Recursion** – A function calls itself directly.
2. **Indirect Recursion** – A function calls another function, which eventually calls the original function.
3. **Tail Recursion** – A recursive function where the recursive call is the last operation before returning a result.

Tail Recursion

Tail recursion is an optimized form of recursion where no computation remains after the recursive call. Some languages (like Haskell and Scala) optimize tail-recursive functions into loops internally.

Example of tail recursion:

```
const factorialTail = (n, acc = 1) => {

  if (n === 0) return acc;

  return factorialTail(n - 1, n * acc);

};



console.log(factorialTail(5)); // 120
```

Here, acc accumulates the result, eliminating the need for extra stack frames.

Tail Recursion in Python (Using `functools.lru_cache`)

```
from functools import lru_cache
```

```python
@lru_cache(None)

def factorial_tail(n, acc=1):

    if n == 0:

        return acc

    return factorial_tail(n - 1, n * acc)



print(factorial_tail(5))   # 120
```

Python does not support tail call optimization, but `lru_cache` can help avoid redundant computations.

Iteration: A Comparison

Iteration is a loop-based approach, where a variable is updated in each iteration until a condition is met.

Example of factorial using iteration:

```javascript
const factorialIterative = (n) => {

  let result = 1;

  for (let i = 1; i <= n; i++) {

    result *= i;

  }

  return result;

};



console.log(factorialIterative(5)); // 120
```

Comparing Recursion and Iteration

Feature	Recursion	Iteration
Readability	More expressive for problems like tree traversal	Straightforward for loops
Memory Usage	Uses stack frames, leading to stack overflow risks	Uses constant memory
Performance	Can be optimized using tail call optimization	Generally faster without optimization
Code Complexity	More concise for divide-and-conquer problems	Easier to understand for simple loops

When to Use Recursion

Recursion is ideal for problems that have a natural recursive structure:

1. **Tree Traversals**
2. **Divide and Conquer Algorithms (Merge Sort, Quick Sort)**
3. **Graph Traversal (DFS)**
4. **Combinatorial Problems (Generating Permutations, Subsets)**

Example: Traversing a binary tree using recursion:

```
class Node {

  constructor(value, left = null, right = null) {

    this.value = value;

    this.left = left;

    this.right = right;

  }

}
```

```
const inOrderTraversal = (node) => {

  if (node === null) return;

  inOrderTraversal(node.left);

  console.log(node.value);

  inOrderTraversal(node.right);

};


const root = new Node(1, new Node(2), new Node(3));

inOrderTraversal(root);   // Output: 2 1 3
```

Optimizing Recursion

1. **Tail Call Optimization (TCO)** – Some languages (Haskell, Scala) automatically optimize tail-recursive calls into loops.
2. **Memoization** – Storing computed results to avoid redundant calls.

Example of memoization in JavaScript:

```
const memoize = (fn) => {

  const cache = {};

  return (n) => {

    if (n in cache) return cache[n];

    return (cache[n] = fn(n));

  };

};
```

```
const factorialMemoized = memoize((n) => (n === 0 ? 1 : n *
factorialMemoized(n - 1)));


console.log(factorialMemoized(5));  // 120
```

Conclusion

Both recursion and iteration have their use cases in functional programming. Recursion provides a more natural way to express problems like tree traversals and divide-and-conquer algorithms, while iteration is more memory-efficient and preferred for simple loops. Understanding these techniques helps in writing more efficient and readable functional code.

Lazy Evaluation and Its Benefits

Lazy evaluation is a powerful technique in functional programming that delays the computation of expressions until their results are actually needed. This approach can improve performance by avoiding unnecessary calculations, optimizing memory usage, and enabling the creation of infinite data structures.

Understanding Lazy Evaluation

In eager evaluation (strict evaluation), expressions are evaluated as soon as they are bound to a variable. In contrast, lazy evaluation defers computation until the value is required. This can be useful in reducing redundant calculations and improving efficiency in programs.

For example, consider the following eager evaluation approach:

```
const square = x => x * x;

const result = square(5) + square(6);  // Both square(5) and square(6)
are evaluated immediately

console.log(result); // 61
```

In a lazily evaluated environment, the computation of `square(5)` and `square(6)` would only take place if and when `result` is used.

Lazy Evaluation in Functional Languages

Many functional languages, like Haskell, use lazy evaluation by default. This allows infinite data structures and efficient handling of computations that might never be needed.

Example in Haskell

```
ones :: [Int]

ones = 1 : ones   -- Infinite list of ones


take 5 ones   -- [1,1,1,1,1]
```

Even though ones is an infinite list, Haskell only evaluates the first five elements when needed.

Implementing Lazy Evaluation in JavaScript

JavaScript does not support lazy evaluation by default, but it can be implemented using generators or higher-order functions.

Using Generators

```
function* lazyRange(start = 1) {

  let num = start;

  while (true) {

    yield num++;

  }

}


const numbers = lazyRange();

console.log(numbers.next().value); // 1

console.log(numbers.next().value); // 2
```

```
console.log(numbers.next().value); // 3
```

Here, the generator function `lazyRange` produces an infinite sequence but only computes values when requested.

Lazy Map Implementation

We can also implement a lazily evaluated `map` function:

```
function* lazyMap(iterable, fn) {

  for (const item of iterable) {

    yield fn(item);

  }

}


const numbersGen = lazyRange(1);

const squaredNumbers = lazyMap(numbersGen, x => x * x);


console.log(squaredNumbers.next().value); // 1

console.log(squaredNumbers.next().value); // 4

console.log(squaredNumbers.next().value); // 9
```

Benefits of Lazy Evaluation

1. **Performance Optimization**
   - Computations are only performed when necessary.
   - Reduces redundant evaluations in programs.
2. **Efficient Memory Usage**
   - Prevents unnecessary storage of large intermediate results.
   - Enables working with infinite data structures.
3. **Improved Code Readability**
   - Expressions are evaluated in a natural and declarative manner.

- ○ Avoids unnecessary complexity in data transformations.
4. **Infinite Data Structures**
   - ○ Supports operations on potentially unbounded sequences.
   - ○ Avoids unnecessary computation of unused values.

Infinite Sequences and Streams

Lazy evaluation is essential for working with infinite sequences, as seen in functional programming languages.

Infinite Fibonacci Sequence (JavaScript)

```javascript
function* fibonacci() {

  let [a, b] = [0, 1];

  while (true) {

    yield a;

    [a, b] = [b, a + b];

  }

}


const fib = fibonacci();

console.log(fib.next().value); // 0

console.log(fib.next().value); // 1

console.log(fib.next().value); // 1

console.log(fib.next().value); // 2

console.log(fib.next().value); // 3
```

This generator produces Fibonacci numbers indefinitely without unnecessary computations.

Real-World Applications of Lazy Evaluation

Data Processing Pipelines

Lazy evaluation can optimize data processing, especially when handling large datasets.

```
const        processLargeData        =        lazyMap(fetchLargeDataset(),
transformFunction);
```

Here, `fetchLargeDataset` retrieves a large dataset, but `transformFunction` is only applied as needed.

Functional Reactive Programming (FRP)

Lazy evaluation is commonly used in FRP to manage event-driven computations efficiently.

Example using RxJS:

```
import { fromEvent } from "rxjs";

import { map, filter } from "rxjs/operators";



const keyPresses = fromEvent(document, 'keydown').pipe(

  map(event => event.key),

  filter(key => key === 'Enter')

);



keyPresses.subscribe(key => console.log(`You pressed: ${key}`));
```

Here, the event stream is evaluated lazily, processing only when a keypress occurs.

Trade-offs of Lazy Evaluation

Advantage	Disadvantage

Saves memory by not computing unused values	Can increase execution time due to delayed computation
Enables infinite data structures	Harder to debug due to deferred execution
Improves efficiency in functional pipelines	May introduce unexpected performance issues if misused

Conclusion

Lazy evaluation is a core concept in functional programming that enhances performance, optimizes memory usage, and allows infinite data structures. By deferring computations until they are actually required, it improves efficiency in data processing and stream operations. While it has trade-offs, when used effectively, lazy evaluation can lead to cleaner, more efficient, and more scalable functional code.

Pattern Matching and Destructuring

Pattern matching and destructuring are powerful features in functional programming that allow developers to extract values from complex data structures in a clean and expressive way. These techniques enable declarative and concise code, making data manipulation more intuitive.

Understanding Pattern Matching

Pattern matching is a mechanism for checking a value against a pattern and deconstructing it accordingly. Many functional languages, such as Haskell, Scala, and Elixir, have built-in support for pattern matching, whereas JavaScript and Python offer destructuring as a more limited but still powerful alternative.

Pattern Matching in Functional Programming

Pattern matching allows defining functions and control flow structures based on specific data patterns.

Example in Haskell:

```
factorial :: Integer -> Integer

factorial 0 = 1
```

```
factorial n = n * factorial (n - 1)
```

```
main = print (factorial 5) -- 120
```

Here, `factorial` has two pattern-matched cases:

- When n is 0, it returns 1 (base case).
- Otherwise, it recursively calls itself.

Pattern Matching in Different Languages

Pattern Matching in Scala

Scala has built-in pattern matching using `match` expressions:

```
def describe(x: Any): String = x match {

  case 0 => "zero"

  case 1 => "one"

  case "hello" => "a greeting"

  case _ => "something else"

}
```

```
println(describe(0))       // "zero"

println(describe("hello")) // "a greeting"

println(describe(5))       // "something else"
```

The underscore (_) is a wildcard matching any value.

Pattern Matching in Elixir

Elixir has a powerful pattern matching system:

```
defmodule Math do

  def factorial(0), do: 1

  def factorial(n), do: n * factorial(n - 1)

end



IO.puts Math.factorial(5)  # 120
```

Destructuring: A Practical Alternative

Destructuring is a way to extract values from arrays, tuples, and objects in languages that do not have full pattern matching.

Destructuring Arrays in JavaScript

```
const [first, second, ...rest] = [10, 20, 30, 40, 50];

console.log(first);  // 10

console.log(second); // 20

console.log(rest);   // [30, 40, 50]
```

Here, `first` and `second` extract the first two values, while `rest` collects the remaining values.

Destructuring Objects in JavaScript

```
const person = { name: "Alice", age: 30, city: "New York" };

const { name, age } = person;



console.log(name); // "Alice"
```

```
console.log(age);   // 30
```

This technique simplifies working with object properties.

Destructuring in Python

Python's tuple unpacking achieves similar results:

```
a, b, *rest = (10, 20, 30, 40, 50)

print(a)     # 10
print(b)     # 20
print(rest)  # [30, 40, 50]
```

Python also supports dictionary unpacking:

```
person = { "name": "Alice", "age": 30 }
name, age = person.values()

print(name)  # "Alice"
print(age)   # 30
```

Pattern Matching in Control Flow

Pattern matching simplifies control structures, replacing verbose `if-else` or `switch` statements.

Example in JavaScript (using destructuring):

```
const getStatus = ({ role }) => {
```

```
  switch (role) {

    case "admin":

      return "Administrator Access";

    case "user":

      return "User Access";

    default:

      return "Guest Access";

  }

};


console.log(getStatus({ role: "admin" })); // "Administrator Access"
```

Example in Python (using `match-case` **from Python 3.10):**

```python
def describe(value):

    match value:

        case 0:

            return "zero"

        case 1:

            return "one"

        case "hello":

            return "a greeting"

        case _:

            return "something else"
```

```
print(describe(0))      # "zero"

print(describe("hello")) # "a greeting"

print(describe(5))      # "something else"
```

Real-World Applications of Pattern Matching

1. Parsing JSON Data

Pattern matching and destructuring make JSON parsing cleaner.

Example in JavaScript:

```javascript
const user = { id: 1, name: "Alice", address: { city: "New York" } };


const { name, address: { city } } = user;


console.log(name); // "Alice"

console.log(city); // "New York"
```

2. Functional Error Handling

Pattern matching simplifies error handling.

Example in Scala:

```scala
def safeDivide(x: Int, y: Int): Either[String, Int] =
  if (y == 0) Left("Cannot divide by zero") else Right(x / y)


val result = safeDivide(10, 0) match {
```

```
  case Left(error) => s"Error: $error"

  case Right(value) => s"Result: $value"

}



println(result)  // "Error: Cannot divide by zero"
```

3. Extracting Data in Functional Pipelines

Pattern matching integrates seamlessly in data pipelines.

Example in JavaScript:

```
const users = [

  { id: 1, name: "Alice", role: "admin" },

  { id: 2, name: "Bob", role: "user" }

];



const getAdmins = users => users.filter(({ role }) => role ===
"admin");



console.log(getAdmins(users)); // [{ id: 1, name: "Alice", role:
"admin" }]
```

Performance Considerations

1. **Efficiency** – Pattern matching is often optimized in compiled languages but can introduce overhead in interpreted languages.
2. **Readability** – Improves code clarity by removing unnecessary conditionals.
3. **Maintainability** – Easier to extend when handling multiple data structures.

Conclusion

Pattern matching and destructuring enhance functional programming by providing a concise and declarative way to work with data. These techniques improve readability, reduce redundancy, and make complex control flows more intuitive. Understanding how to leverage them effectively can lead to cleaner, more efficient, and maintainable functional code.

Chapter 4: Working with Data in Functional Programming

Functional Data Structures and Their Properties

Functional programming emphasizes immutability and pure functions, which directly influence how data structures are designed and used. Functional data structures provide efficient, immutable operations that facilitate predictable and bug-free code. These structures are widely used in functional languages like Haskell, Scala, and Clojure but can also be employed in JavaScript and Python.

Characteristics of Functional Data Structures

Functional data structures differ from their imperative counterparts in the following ways:

1. **Immutability** – Functional data structures do not change after they are created. Instead of modifying existing data, operations return new structures.
2. **Persistence** – Previous versions of a data structure remain accessible after modifications.
3. **Structural Sharing** – To optimize memory usage, new structures share parts of the old structure.
4. **Lazy Evaluation** – Many functional data structures evaluate elements only when accessed.

Immutable Lists

Lists are a fundamental data structure in functional programming. Unlike mutable arrays, immutable lists do not allow direct modification.

Immutable List in JavaScript

JavaScript lacks built-in support for immutable lists, but we can create them using recursion:

```
const List = (head, tail = null) => ({ head, tail });


const prepend = (element, list) => List(element, list);


const printList = (list) => {

  if (!list) return;
```

```
  console.log(list.head);

  printList(list.tail);

};
```

```
const numbers = prepend(1, prepend(2, prepend(3, null)));

printList(numbers);

// Output:

// 1

// 2

// 3
```

Here, `prepend` creates a new list instead of modifying the existing one.

Immutable Lists in Haskell

Haskell natively supports immutable lists:

```
numbers = [1, 2, 3, 4, 5]
```

Appending an element creates a new list:

```
newNumbers = 0 : numbers
```

Persistent Data Structures

Persistent data structures retain old versions after modification, ensuring that previous states remain accessible.

Persistent List in JavaScript

We can implement a persistent list using structural sharing:

```
const append = (list, value) => {

  if (!list) return List(value);

  return List(list.head, append(list.tail, value));

};
```

```
const original = prepend(1, prepend(2, null));

const updated = append(original, 3);
```

```
printList(updated); // 1, 2, 3

printList(original); // 1, 2
```

The append function creates a new list instead of altering original, ensuring persistence.

Functional Trees

Trees are widely used in functional programming due to their efficiency and persistence.

Immutable Binary Tree in JavaScript

```
const Tree = (value, left = null, right = null) => ({ value, left,
right });
```

```
const insert = (tree, value) => {

  if (!tree) return Tree(value);

  return value < tree.value

    ? Tree(tree.value, insert(tree.left, value), tree.right)

    : Tree(tree.value, tree.left, insert(tree.right, value));
```

```
};
```

```
const tree = insert(null, 10);

const tree2 = insert(tree, 5);

const tree3 = insert(tree2, 15);

console.log(tree3);
```

Here, each insertion creates a new tree instead of modifying the original.

Tree Traversal in Haskell

```
data Tree a = Empty | Node a (Tree a) (Tree a) deriving Show


insert :: Ord a => a -> Tree a -> Tree a

insert x Empty = Node x Empty Empty

insert x (Node y left right)

    | x < y = Node y (insert x left) right

    | otherwise = Node y left (insert x right)


tree = insert 10 (insert 5 (insert 15 Empty))
```

This ensures that previous versions of the tree remain accessible.

Functional Maps (Dictionaries)

Maps (or dictionaries) store key-value pairs and are useful in functional programming.

Persistent Map in JavaScript

Using the Map object, we can implement an immutable dictionary:

```
const updateMap = (map, key, value) => new Map([...map, [key,
value]]);
```

```
const originalMap = new Map([["name", "Alice"]]);
```

```
const updatedMap = updateMap(originalMap, "age", 30);
```

```
console.log(originalMap); // Map { "name" => "Alice" }
```

```
console.log(updatedMap);  // Map { "name" => "Alice", "age" => 30 }
```

The updateMap function returns a new map with the added key-value pair.

Functional Sets

Sets are collections of unique elements.

Immutable Sets in JavaScript

```
const addToSet = (set, value) => new Set([...set, value]);
```

```
const originalSet = new Set([1, 2, 3]);
```

```
const updatedSet = addToSet(originalSet, 4);
```

```
console.log(originalSet); // Set {1, 2, 3}
```

```
console.log(updatedSet);  // Set {1, 2, 3, 4}
```

Comparing Functional and Imperative Data Structures

Feature	Functional (Immutable)	Imperative (Mutable)
Modification	Creates new structure	Modifies in-place
Memory Usage	Optimized via sharing	Uses direct memory
Concurrency	Safe due to immutability	Requires locking mechanisms
Complexity	More initial learning	Easier for beginners

Real-World Applications

1. **Versioned Data Stores** – Persistent data structures enable storing multiple versions of a dataset.
2. **Undo/Redo Functionality** – Applications like text editors rely on immutable structures.
3. **Concurrency and Parallelism** – Immutability ensures thread-safe operations.

Conclusion

Functional data structures play a critical role in functional programming, enabling immutability, persistence, and structural sharing. Understanding these structures allows developers to write efficient, maintainable, and predictable functional code.

Persistent Data Structures and Their Use Cases

Persistent data structures are a crucial concept in functional programming, enabling immutability while maintaining efficiency. Unlike mutable data structures, which change state in place, persistent data structures preserve previous versions of themselves when modified. This makes them highly suitable for functional programming, where immutability is a fundamental principle.

Understanding Persistence in Data Structures

A data structure is **persistent** if previous versions remain accessible after updates. There are three types of persistence:

1. **Partial Persistence** – Only the most recent version can be modified, but older versions remain accessible.
2. **Full Persistence** – Any version can be modified, and all versions are accessible.
3. **Confluent Persistence** – Multiple versions can be combined to create new versions.

Many functional languages, such as Haskell, Clojure, and Scala, provide built-in support for persistent data structures.

Structural Sharing in Persistent Data Structures

Persistent data structures avoid redundant copying by using **structural sharing**—a technique where new versions of a structure share unchanged parts with previous versions.

Consider the following example:

```
const oldArray = [1, 2, 3];

const newArray = [...oldArray, 4];  // Creates a new array instead of
modifying the old one


console.log(oldArray); // [1, 2, 3]

console.log(newArray); // [1, 2, 3, 4]
```

Here, `oldArray` remains unchanged while `newArray` extends it.

Persistent Lists

Lists are a fundamental data structure in functional programming. Persistent lists maintain their previous versions when updated.

Persistent List in JavaScript

Since JavaScript lacks native persistent data structures, we can implement an immutable list manually:

```
const List = (head, tail = null) => ({ head, tail });


const prepend = (element, list) => List(element, list);


const numbers = prepend(1, prepend(2, prepend(3, null)));
```

```
console.log(numbers);

// { head: 1, tail: { head: 2, tail: { head: 3, tail: null } } }
```

Each prepend operation returns a new list without modifying the original.

Persistent List in Haskell

Haskell natively supports immutable lists:

```
numbers = [1, 2, 3]

newNumbers = 0 : numbers    -- Adds 0 to the front, preserving the
original list
```

Persistent Trees

Trees are widely used in functional programming due to their efficiency and structural sharing.

Persistent Binary Tree in JavaScript

```
const Tree = (value, left = null, right = null) => ({ value, left,
right });


const insert = (tree, value) => {

  if (!tree) return Tree(value);

  return value < tree.value

    ? Tree(tree.value, insert(tree.left, value), tree.right)

    : Tree(tree.value, tree.left, insert(tree.right, value));

};
```

```
const tree = insert(null, 10);

const tree2 = insert(tree, 5);

const tree3 = insert(tree2, 15);


console.log(tree3);
```

This ensures that previous versions of tree remain unchanged.

Persistent Tree in Haskell

```
data Tree a = Empty | Node a (Tree a) (Tree a) deriving Show


insert :: Ord a => a -> Tree a -> Tree a
insert x Empty = Node x Empty Empty
insert x (Node y left right)
    | x < y = Node y (insert x left) right
    | otherwise = Node y left (insert x right)


tree = insert 10 (insert 5 (insert 15 Empty))
```

Each modification creates a new version of the tree.

Persistent Hash Maps (Dictionaries)

Dictionaries are widely used in programming for key-value storage. Functional programming offers persistent alternatives.

Persistent Map in JavaScript

```
const updateMap = (map, key, value) => new Map([...map, [key,
value]]);
```

```
const originalMap = new Map([["name", "Alice"]]);
```

```
const updatedMap = updateMap(originalMap, "age", 30);
```

```
console.log(originalMap); // Map { "name" => "Alice" }
```

```
console.log(updatedMap);  // Map { "name" => "Alice", "age" => 30 }
```

Instead of modifying originalMap, updateMap returns a new version.

Persistent Sets

Sets store unique elements. Functional programming ensures immutability in sets.

Persistent Set in JavaScript

```
const addToSet = (set, value) => new Set([...set, value]);
```

```
const originalSet = new Set([1, 2, 3]);
```

```
const updatedSet = addToSet(originalSet, 4);
```

```
console.log(originalSet); // Set {1, 2, 3}
```

```
console.log(updatedSet);  // Set {1, 2, 3, 4}
```

Performance Considerations

Feature	Persistent Structures	Data Mutable Data Structures

Immutability	Preserves old versions	Overwrites data
Structural Sharing	Reuses memory	Copies data
Concurrency	Thread-safe	Requires locking
Performance	May have overhead	Faster in-place updates

Real-World Applications

1. **Version Control Systems** – Persistent data structures enable tracking of changes over time.
2. **Undo/Redo Features** – Applications like text editors rely on persistence.
3. **Functional Databases** – Immutable databases ensure data consistency.
4. **Concurrency Management** – Enables thread-safe operations in parallel computing.

Conclusion

Persistent data structures are a cornerstone of functional programming, enabling immutability, efficiency, and structural sharing. Understanding these structures allows developers to write scalable and maintainable functional code.

Functional Error Handling: Option, Either, and Try Monads

Error handling is a critical part of software development, and functional programming offers a different approach compared to traditional imperative error handling mechanisms like exceptions. Instead of relying on side effects and throwing exceptions, functional programming emphasizes using monadic structures like `Option`, `Either`, and `Try` to handle errors in a composable and predictable manner.

The Problem with Traditional Error Handling

In imperative programming, error handling often relies on exceptions:

```
function divide(a, b) {
  if (b === 0) {
```

```
      throw new Error("Division by zero");

  }

  return a / b;

}


try {

  console.log(divide(10, 0));

} catch (error) {

  console.error("Error:", error.message);

}
```

While exceptions work, they introduce side effects and make reasoning about code more difficult. Functional programming replaces exceptions with explicit return types.

The Option Monad

The Option monad represents the presence (Some(value)) or absence (None) of a value. This helps avoid null or undefined errors.

Implementing Option in JavaScript

```
class Option {

  constructor(value) {

    this.value = value;

  }


  static Some(value) {

    return new Option(value);
```

```
  }


  static None() {

    return new Option(null);

  }


  map(fn) {

    return    this.value    ===    null   ?    Option.None()    :
Option.Some(fn(this.value));

  }


  getOrElse(defaultValue) {

    return this.value === null ? defaultValue : this.value;

  }

}


const safeDivide = (a, b) =>

  b === 0 ? Option.None() : Option.Some(a / b);


console.log(safeDivide(10, 2).getOrElse("Error")); // 5

console.log(safeDivide(10, 0).getOrElse("Error")); // "Error"
```

Here, Option replaces null checks and makes it clear whether a value exists.

Option in Scala

Scala has a built-in Option type:

```
def safeDivide(a: Int, b: Int): Option[Int] =

  if (b == 0) None else Some(a / b)
```

```
println(safeDivide(10, 2).getOrElse("Error")) // 5

println(safeDivide(10, 0).getOrElse("Error")) // "Error"
```

The Either Monad

The `Either` monad represents two possible outcomes:

- `Left(value)`: Represents an error.
- `Right(value)`: Represents a successful result.

Implementing Either in JavaScript

```
class Either {

  constructor(left, right) {

    this.left = left;

    this.right = right;

  }


  static Left(value) {

    return new Either(value, null);

  }


  static Right(value) {

    return new Either(null, value);
```

```
    }


    map(fn) {

        return this.right === null ? this : Either.Right(fn(this.right));

    }


    getOrElse(defaultValue) {

        return this.right === null ? defaultValue : this.right;

    }

}


const safeDivide = (a, b) =>

    b === 0 ? Either.Left("Cannot divide by zero") : Either.Right(a /
b);


console.log(safeDivide(10, 2).getOrElse("Error")); // 5

console.log(safeDivide(10, 0).getOrElse("Error")); // "Cannot divide
by zero"
```

Either in Scala

Scala's Either type is widely used in functional programming:

```
def safeDivide(a: Int, b: Int): Either[String, Int] =

    if (b == 0) Left("Cannot divide by zero") else Right(a / b)
```

```
println(safeDivide(10, 2).getOrElse("Error")) // 5

println(safeDivide(10, 0).getOrElse("Error")) // "Cannot divide by
zero"
```

The Try Monad

The `Try` monad is useful for handling exceptions while keeping computations pure. It represents:

- `Success(value)`: A successful computation.
- `Failure(error)`: An exception.

Implementing Try in JavaScript

```
class Try {

  constructor(fn) {

    try {

      this.value = fn();

      this.success = true;

    } catch (error) {

      this.value = error;

      this.success = false;

    }

  }


  map(fn) {

    return this.success ? new Try(() => fn(this.value)) : this;

  }
```

```
getOrElse(defaultValue) {

    return this.success ? this.value : defaultValue;

  }

}
```

```
const safeParseJson = (json) => new Try(() => JSON.parse(json));
```

```
console.log(safeParseJson('{"name":    "Alice"}').getOrElse("Invalid
JSON")); // { name: "Alice" }
```

```
console.log(safeParseJson("Invalid").getOrElse("Invalid  JSON")); //
"Invalid JSON"
```

Try in Scala

Scala has a built-in Try type:

```
import scala.util.{Try, Success, Failure}
```

```
def safeParseJson(json: String): Try[Map[String, String]] = Try {

  import scala.util.parsing.json.JSON

  JSON.parseFull(json).get.asInstanceOf[Map[String, String]]

}
```

```
println(safeParseJson("""{"name":    "Alice"}""").getOrElse("Invalid
JSON"))
```

```
println(safeParseJson("Invalid").getOrElse("Invalid JSON"))
```

Comparing Option, Either, and Try

Feature	Option	Either	Try
Represents missing values	✓	✗	✗
Represents errors	✗	✓	✓
Supports error messages	✗	✓	✓
Handles exceptions	✗	✗	✓

Functional Error Handling in Real-World Applications

1. **API Responses** – Handle success and error responses without throwing exceptions.
2. **Configuration Management** – Avoid crashes due to missing values.
3. **Data Parsing** – Handle invalid inputs gracefully.
4. **Database Queries** – Ensure safe query execution.

Conclusion

Functional programming provides structured ways to handle errors through `Option`, `Either`, and `Try`. These monads allow handling errors in a composable, predictable manner, making functional code more robust and maintainable.

Handling Side Effects with Pure Functional Approaches

Functional programming emphasizes **purity**, meaning functions should not have side effects. However, real-world applications must interact with the outside world—reading files, making HTTP requests, logging data, and modifying state. Functional programming provides ways to handle side effects while maintaining purity, ensuring that functions remain composable and predictable.

Understanding Side Effects

A **side effect** occurs when a function interacts with the outside world or modifies state outside its scope. Examples include:

- Modifying global variables
- Mutating objects or arrays
- Performing I/O operations (logging, file reading/writing)
- Making network requests
- Generating random numbers

For example, in imperative programming:

```
let counter = 0;

function increment() {

   counter += 1;

}

increment();

console.log(counter); // 1
```

Here, `increment` modifies the external `counter` variable, making it impure.

In functional programming, we aim to eliminate or isolate side effects.

Pure vs. Impure Functions

A **pure function**:

1. Always returns the same output for the same input.
2. Has no observable side effects.

Example of a **pure function**:

```
const add = (a, b) => a + b;

console.log(add(2, 3)); // 5
```

Example of an **impure function**:

```
let total = 0;


function addToTotal(value) {

  total += value;

}


addToTotal(5);

console.log(total); // 5 (mutated external state)
```

Strategies for Handling Side Effects

Functional programming offers techniques to handle side effects while keeping functions pure:

1. **Encapsulation Using Higher-Order Functions**
2. **Monads (IO Monad, State Monad)**
3. **Referential Transparency with Deferred Execution**
4. **Immutable Data Structures**
5. **Effect Systems (like Eff and ZIO in Scala)**

1. Encapsulation Using Higher-Order Functions

Side effects can be encapsulated within higher-order functions, ensuring that core logic remains pure.

Example: Wrapping side effects in a function:

```
const log = (message) => () => console.log(message);


const logMessage = log("Hello, Functional Programming!");

logMessage(); // Logs "Hello, Functional Programming!"
```

Here, `log` returns a function that performs the side effect when explicitly called.

2. Using the IO Monad to Defer Execution

Monads help manage side effects in a controlled way. The **IO Monad** encapsulates side effects without executing them immediately.

IO Monad in JavaScript

```
class IO {

  constructor(effect) {

    this.effect = effect;

  }


  map(fn) {

    return new IO(() => fn(this.effect()));

  }


  run() {

    return this.effect();

  }

}


const getTime = new IO(() => new Date().toISOString());

const logTime = getTime.map(time => `Current Time: ${time}`);


console.log(logTime.run()); // Executes the side effect
```

Here, `getTime` is a **pure function** that returns an IO instance. The actual effect is only executed when `run()` is called.

IO Monad in Haskell

```haskell
main :: IO ()

main = do

    time <- getCurrentTime

    putStrLn ("Current time: " ++ show time)
```

The effect is controlled and executed within the `IO` monad.

3. Referential Transparency with Deferred Execution

Referential transparency ensures that an expression can be replaced with its evaluated result without changing program behavior.

Example:

```javascript
const random = () => Math.random(); // Impure
```

To make it pure, we can defer execution:

```javascript
const randomEffect = () => () => Math.random();

const getRandom = randomEffect();
```

```javascript
console.log(getRandom()); // Generates a random number
```

4. Immutable Data Structures for Side Effects

Instead of mutating objects, use immutable updates:

Using Spread Operator (JavaScript)

```javascript
const updateUser = (user, newName) => ({ ...user, name: newName });


const user = { id: 1, name: "Alice" };
const updatedUser = updateUser(user, "Bob");


console.log(user); // { id: 1, name: "Alice" } (original remains
unchanged)
console.log(updatedUser); // { id: 1, name: "Bob" }
```

5. Effect Systems for Pure Side Effects

Some functional languages offer advanced **effect systems** to control side effects:

- **Eff** (PureScript)
- **ZIO** (Scala) – Handles effects using fibers (lightweight threads)
- **Cats Effect** (Scala) – Functional concurrency management

Example in **ZIO (Scala)**:

```scala
import zio._


val program = for {

  _     <- Console.printLine("Enter your name:")

  name <- Console.readLine

  _     <- Console.printLine(s"Hello, $name!")
} yield ()
```

```
@main def run() = Runtime.default.unsafeRun(program)
```

Effects are wrapped in ZIO monads and executed safely.

Real-World Applications of Functional Side Effects

1. **Logging Without Polluting Core Logic**
   - Encapsulating log functions ensures purity.
2. **Lazy Loading and Memoization**
   - Ensuring expensive computations execute only when needed.
3. **Managing Asynchronous Operations**
   - Using Promises or async functions without breaking purity.
4. **State Management in UI Frameworks**
   - Frameworks like Redux use **pure reducers**.

Conclusion

Functional programming isolates side effects while keeping the core logic pure. Using IO monads, immutable data structures, and controlled execution, developers can maintain predictable and maintainable code while interacting with the real world.

Streams and Pipelines in Data Processing

Streams and pipelines are fundamental concepts in functional programming that allow efficient, composable, and lazy data processing. These techniques enable handling large datasets, optimizing memory usage, and improving performance by processing data incrementally rather than loading everything into memory at once.

Understanding Streams

A **stream** is a sequence of data elements made available over time. Unlike arrays, which store data in memory, streams generate and process data **lazily**, meaning values are produced on demand.

Streams can be finite (e.g., reading a file line by line) or infinite (e.g., generating an unbounded sequence of numbers).

Example: Stream vs. Array in JavaScript

```
const numbersArray = [1, 2, 3, 4, 5]; // All elements stored in memory

console.log(numbersArray.map(n => n * 2)); // [2, 4, 6, 8, 10]
```

```javascript
// Stream-like processing using a generator

function* numberStream() {

  let num = 1;

  while (true) {

    yield num++;

  }

}


const stream = numberStream();

console.log(stream.next().value); // 1

console.log(stream.next().value); // 2

console.log(stream.next().value); // 3
```

Here, `numberStream` generates numbers lazily, consuming memory only when needed.

Benefits of Streams

1. **Efficient Memory Usage** – Streams process data incrementally instead of storing entire datasets in memory.
2. **Improved Performance** – Streaming prevents unnecessary computations, reducing processing time.
3. **Composable Data Transformation** – Stream transformations (mapping, filtering, reducing) can be combined into efficient data pipelines.
4. **Handles Infinite Data** – Streams enable working with potentially infinite sequences.

Functional Pipelines

A **pipeline** is a sequence of functions applied to data in a structured manner. Pipelines allow composing multiple transformations without mutating the original data.

Example: Pipeline in JavaScript

```javascript
const double = x => x * 2;
```

```
const increment = x => x + 1;

const toString = x => `Number: ${x}`;



const pipeline = (x) => toString(increment(double(x)));



console.log(pipeline(5)); // "Number: 11"
```

Pipelines make data transformation **clear, readable, and modular**.

Stream Processing in Functional Languages

Streams in JavaScript Using RxJS

RxJS (Reactive Extensions for JavaScript) provides a powerful way to handle asynchronous data streams.

```
import { fromEvent } from "rxjs";

import { map, filter } from "rxjs/operators";



const clicks = fromEvent(document, 'click').pipe(

  map(event => event.clientX),

  filter(x => x > 200)

);



clicks.subscribe(x => console.log(`Clicked at: ${x}`));
```

Here, we listen for `click` events, extract the X coordinate, filter clicks on the right side of the screen, and log the results.

Streams in Python Using Itertools

Python's `itertools` module provides functional tools for stream processing:

```python
from itertools import count, islice

stream = count(1)  # Infinite sequence: 1, 2, 3, ...

first_ten = list(islice(stream, 10))
print(first_ten)  # [1, 2, 3, 4, 5, 6, 7, 8, 9, 10]
```

Streams in Haskell

Haskell uses lazy evaluation, making streams (infinite lists) natural:

```haskell
numbers = [1..]  -- Infinite list of numbers

take 5 numbers  -- [1, 2, 3, 4, 5]
```

Haskell processes only the necessary elements instead of computing the entire list.

Data Transformation with Pipelines

Pipelines efficiently transform and process streamed data.

Example: Processing a Large Dataset in JavaScript

```javascript
const users = [
  { name: "Alice", age: 25 },
  { name: "Bob", age: 30 },
  { name: "Charlie", age: 35 }
```

```
];
```

```
const transform = users
  .filter(user => user.age > 25)
  .map(user => user.name.toUpperCase());
```

```
console.log(transform); // ["BOB", "CHARLIE"]
```

This pipeline:

1. Filters users older than 25.
2. Converts their names to uppercase.

Example: Processing a Text File Line-by-Line in Python

```python
def process_file(filename):
    with open(filename, 'r') as file:
        for line in file:
            yield line.strip().upper()
```

```python
for line in process_file("data.txt"):
    print(line)
```

Instead of loading the whole file into memory, this function processes one line at a time.

Combining Streams and Pipelines

Streams and pipelines work together to process large or infinite datasets efficiently.

Example: Combining Streams and Pipelines in JavaScript

```
function* generateNumbers() {

  let num = 1;

  while (true) yield num++;

}


const pipeline = (stream) => {

  return stream

    .map(n => n * 2)

    .filter(n => n % 3 === 0)

    .slice(0, 5);

};


console.log([...pipeline(generateNumbers())]); // First 5 numbers
divisible by 3
```

This pipeline:

1. Doubles numbers.
2. Filters those divisible by 3.
3. Extracts the first five results.

Error Handling in Streams

Since streams process data lazily, handling errors properly is essential.

Handling Errors in JavaScript Streams

```
import { of } from "rxjs";

import { map, catchError } from "rxjs/operators";
```

```
const dataStream = of(1, 2, 3, "error", 5).pipe(

  map(x => {

    if (typeof x !== "number") throw new Error("Invalid data");

    return x * 2;

  }),

  catchError(err => {

    console.error(err.message);

    return of(null);  // Return a default value

  })

);



dataStream.subscribe(console.log);
```

Comparing Streams vs. Traditional Data Processing

Feature	Streams	Traditional (Arrays)
Memory Usage	Low (lazy processing)	High (stores all data)
Performance	Optimized	Can be slow for large datasets
Composability	High (chaining transformations)	Moderate
Handles Infinite Data	Yes	No

Real-World Applications

1. **Real-Time Data Processing** – Streams handle data in messaging queues like Kafka.
2. **Functional UI Programming** – Reactive programming in frameworks like React and RxJS.
3. **Large-Scale Data Analysis** – Pipeline-based transformations in big data tools.

Conclusion

Streams and pipelines allow efficient, lazy data processing in functional programming. By structuring transformations as composable operations, they enable memory-efficient and scalable data handling, making them ideal for real-world applications.

Chapter 5: Key Functional Programming Paradigms and Concepts

Declarative vs. Imperative Thinking

When discussing programming paradigms, two fundamental approaches emerge: **declarative** and **imperative** programming. These paradigms dictate how programmers express logic and structure within their applications. While imperative programming focuses on *how* things are done, step by step, declarative programming emphasizes *what* should be achieved, allowing the underlying system to determine the execution details.

Understanding Imperative Programming

Imperative programming is the traditional approach to software development. It involves giving the computer a sequence of instructions that manipulate the program's state directly. Most mainstream programming languages, including C, Java, and Python, initially embraced this style. Key characteristics of imperative programming include:

- **Explicit control flow:** The developer defines exact steps the program must follow.
- **Mutable state:** Variables are reassigned throughout execution.
- **Statements over expressions:** Code execution relies on sequential operations.
- **Loops and conditional branching:** Constructs like `for`, `while`, and `if-else` drive logic.

For example, an imperative approach to summing a list of numbers in Python might look like this:

```python
numbers = [1, 2, 3, 4, 5]

total = 0

for num in numbers:

    total += num

print(total)  # Output: 15
```

This example explicitly defines how the summation occurs, modifying `total` at each iteration.

Understanding Declarative Programming

Declarative programming shifts focus from *how* a task is executed to *what* result should be produced. This paradigm allows developers to write code that expresses intent, leaving implementation details to the compiler or interpreter. Common characteristics include:

- **Expression-driven programming:** Computations return values rather than rely on state changes.
- **Reduced side effects:** Functions avoid modifying external variables.
- **Built-in abstractions:** The language provides constructs that encapsulate complex behaviors.

A declarative approach to summing numbers in Python using sum( ) looks like this:

```python
numbers = [1, 2, 3, 4, 5]

total = sum(numbers)

print(total)  # Output: 15
```

Here, the logic is abstracted away; we specify *what* we want (the sum), and Python handles the implementation.

Key Differences Between Imperative and Declarative Programming

Feature	Imperative Programming	Declarative Programming
Control Flow	Explicit, step-by-step	Abstracted, high-level
State Mutability	Mutates variables	Prefers immutability
Code Complexity	Often more verbose	More concise and readable
Side Effects	Common	Minimized
Typical Constructs	Loops, assignments	Map, filter, reduce

Functional Programming as a Declarative Paradigm

Functional programming is a prime example of the declarative paradigm. By emphasizing pure functions, immutability, and composability, it allows developers to write predictable and modular code. Consider a functional approach to summing numbers using `reduce`:

```python
from functools import reduce


numbers = [1, 2, 3, 4, 5]
total = reduce(lambda x, y: x + y, numbers)
print(total)  # Output: 15
```

This approach eliminates explicit iteration and variable mutation, favoring function composition.

Advantages of Declarative Programming

Declarative programming offers several benefits, particularly in functional programming:

1. **Improved Readability:** Code describes intent rather than implementation details.
2. **Easier Maintenance:** Less reliance on state changes reduces debugging complexity.
3. **Better Parallelism:** Pure functions and immutability facilitate concurrency.
4. **Higher-Level Abstractions:** Functions like `map` and `reduce` encapsulate behavior, reducing redundancy.

When to Use Declarative Programming

While declarative programming is powerful, it is not always the best choice. It excels in:

- **Data transformation pipelines** (e.g., functional constructs in JavaScript, Python, and Scala)
- **Concurrency and parallel computing** (e.g., immutable state in Haskell)
- **Database queries** (e.g., SQL, a declarative language)
- **UI development** (e.g., React, which uses a declarative component-based model)

However, low-level system programming and performance-critical applications may still favor imperative programming due to its explicit control over execution.

Conclusion

Declarative and imperative paradigms each have their strengths and weaknesses. While imperative programming remains widely used, functional programming's declarative nature is gaining popularity due to its benefits in maintainability, scalability, and correctness. By embracing declarative techniques, developers can write more expressive, efficient, and robust software.

Algebraic Data Types (ADTs)

Algebraic Data Types (ADTs) are a core concept in functional programming, providing structured and predictable ways to model data. ADTs describe composite types constructed from other types using well-defined rules. These types enforce correctness by ensuring that data adheres to specific structures, making programs more robust and easier to reason about.

ADTs primarily consist of two fundamental types:

1. **Sum Types (Tagged Unions or Variants)** – Represent data that can take one of several distinct forms.
2. **Product Types (Tuples and Records)** – Represent data that combines multiple values into a single structure.

By leveraging ADTs, functional programming languages enforce type safety and eliminate entire classes of runtime errors.

Sum Types (Disjoint Unions)

Sum types, also known as **union types** or **variants**, allow a value to be one of several possible types. This is useful when defining entities that have multiple valid forms but should always belong to one of them.

A classic example of a sum type is defining a Shape type that can be a Circle or a Rectangle:

Example in Haskell:

```
data Shape = Circle Float
         | Rectangle Float Float
```

Here:

- Circle takes a single Float representing the radius.
- Rectangle takes two Float values representing width and height.

Example in Scala:

```scala
sealed trait Shape

case class Circle(radius: Double) extends Shape

case class Rectangle(width: Double, height: Double) extends Shape
```

Example in TypeScript:

```typescript
type Shape =
  | { kind: "circle"; radius: number }
  | { kind: "rectangle"; width: number; height: number };

function area(shape: Shape): number {
  switch (shape.kind) {
    case "circle":
      return Math.PI * shape.radius ** 2;
    case "rectangle":
      return shape.width * shape.height;
  }
}
```

Using **pattern matching**, we can define functions that operate differently depending on the type of the data.

Product Types (Records and Tuples)

Product types allow multiple values to be grouped together into a structured form. Unlike sum types, which define mutually exclusive variants, product types combine multiple fields into a single entity.

A **tuple** is the simplest product type:

Example in Haskell:

```
type Point = (Float, Float)
```

A **record** (or a case class in Scala) provides a named structure:

Example in Scala:

```
case class Person(name: String, age: Int)
```

Example in TypeScript:

```
type Person = {
  name: string;
  age: number;
};
```

Product types are useful for modeling entities with multiple properties that are always present together.

Combining Sum and Product Types

ADTs shine when we **combine sum and product types** to model complex data structures.

Consider modeling a **binary tree**:

Example in Haskell:

```
data Tree a = Leaf a | Node (Tree a) (Tree a)
```

Example in Scala:

```scala
sealed trait Tree[+A]

case class Leaf[A](value: A) extends Tree[A]

case class Node[A](left: Tree[A], right: Tree[A]) extends Tree[A]
```

These definitions enforce that a tree must either be a `Leaf` containing a value or a `Node` containing two subtrees.

Real-World Use Cases

Error Handling: Option and Either Types

Many functional languages provide an **Option** (or **Maybe**) type to handle values that may or may not exist.

Example in Haskell:

```haskell
data Maybe a = Nothing | Just a
```

Example in Scala:

```scala
sealed trait Option[+A]

case class Some[A](value: A) extends Option[A]

case object None extends Option[Nothing]
```

This avoids `null` values and forces explicit handling of missing values.

For error handling, `Either` (or `Result`) is used:

```haskell
data Either a b = Left a | Right b
```

```
sealed trait Either[+A, +B]

case class Left[A](value: A) extends Either[A, Nothing]

case class Right[B](value: B) extends Either[Nothing, B]
```

This models computations that may either return a success (Right) or an error (Left).

Enforcing Exhaustiveness with Pattern Matching

When working with ADTs, **pattern matching** ensures that all possible cases are considered. This prevents runtime errors by forcing developers to handle every variant of a sum type.

Example in Haskell:

```
describeShape :: Shape -> String

describeShape (Circle r) = "A circle with radius " ++ show r

describeShape (Rectangle w h) = "A rectangle of width " ++ show w ++
" and height " ++ show h
```

If a new variant is added to Shape, the compiler will warn about missing cases, improving maintainability.

Benefits of Algebraic Data Types

1. **Type Safety** – Prevents invalid states from existing.
2. **Exhaustiveness Checking** – Enforces handling of all possible cases.
3. **Better Maintainability** – Code is easier to extend and refactor.
4. **Immutability by Default** – Helps with reasoning about program behavior.
5. **Declarative Data Modeling** – Clearly expresses intent in the type system.

ADTs in Non-Functional Languages

Although ADTs are common in purely functional languages like Haskell, they can also be implemented in non-functional languages. TypeScript's discriminated unions and Rust's enum system borrow concepts from ADTs.

Example in Rust:

```rust
enum Shape {

    Circle(f64),

    Rectangle(f64, f64),

}
```

Rust's exhaustive pattern matching ensures safe handling of all cases.

Conclusion

Algebraic Data Types (ADTs) provide a structured way to model data in functional programming. By using sum and product types, developers can create robust, predictable, and maintainable software. The combination of **type safety, pattern matching, and immutability** makes ADTs a crucial tool in modern software design. Whether handling errors, modeling domain entities, or building recursive data structures, ADTs offer a powerful abstraction for managing complexity.

Functors, Applicatives, and Monads Explained

In functional programming, **functors, applicatives, and monads** are fundamental abstractions that enable powerful composition, transformation, and control over computations. These concepts come from category theory and help structure functional code by encapsulating values and defining how functions apply to those values.

Understanding these abstractions is crucial for writing expressive, safe, and reusable functional programs. Each builds on the previous:

1. **Functors** allow applying a function to a wrapped value.
2. **Applicatives** extend functors, enabling functions that are also wrapped to be applied.
3. **Monads** further extend applicatives by handling computations that involve chaining and side effects.

These structures provide a systematic approach to dealing with **optional values, side effects, asynchronous computations, and error handling**.

Functors: Mapping Over Context

A **functor** is a structure that can be mapped over, meaning a function can be applied to a value inside a container without unwrapping it. The most common functor is a **list**, but many other structures—like `Option`, `Result`, and even asynchronous computations—can be functors.

Functor Laws

A functor must obey two laws:

Identity Law: Mapping with an identity function should not change the value.
bash

```
fmap id = id
```

  1.

Composition Law: Mapping over a composition of two functions is the same as mapping them sequentially.
nginx

```
fmap (f . g) = fmap f . fmap g
```

  2.

Example in Haskell

```
class Functor f where

    fmap :: (a -> b) -> f a -> f b
```

```
instance Functor Maybe where

    fmap _ Nothing  = Nothing

    fmap f (Just x) = Just (f x)
```

Example in Scala

```
trait Functor[F[_]] {

  def map[A, B](fa: F[A])(f: A => B): F[B]
```

```
}


implicit val optionFunctor: Functor[Option] = new Functor[Option] {

  def map[A, B](fa: Option[A])(f: A => B): Option[B] = fa match {

    case Some(value) => Some(f(value))

    case None        => None

  }

}
```

Example in JavaScript (for arrays)

```
const numbers = [1, 2, 3];

const doubled = numbers.map(n => n * 2);

console.log(doubled); // [2, 4, 6]
```

The key idea is that a functor provides a consistent way to transform values inside a structure using map.

Applicative Functors: Applying Wrapped Functions

A **functor** allows applying a function to a wrapped value, but what if we have a **wrapped function** we want to apply to a wrapped value? This is where **applicative functors** come in.

Example Problem

Suppose we have:

- Just (x -> x + 2)
- Just 5

How do we apply the function inside Just to Just 5?

Applicative Laws

Identity: Wrapping an identity function should not change the structure.
bash

```
pure id <*> v = v
```

1.

Homomorphism: Applying a function inside a structure should be the same as applying it normally.
java

```
pure f <*> pure x = pure (f x)
```

2.

Interchange: The order of application should not matter.
java

```
u <*> pure y = pure ($ y) <*> u
```

3.

Composition: Nested function application should work.
markdown

```
pure (.) <*> u <*> v <*> w = u <*> (v <*> w)
```

4.

Example in Haskell

```
class Functor f => Applicative f where

    pure :: a -> f a

    (<*>) :: f (a -> b) -> f a -> f b


instance Applicative Maybe where

    pure = Just

    Nothing <*> _ = Nothing
```

```
(Just f) <*> something = fmap f something
```

Example in Scala

```scala
trait Applicative[F[_]] extends Functor[F] {

  def pure[A](a: A): F[A]

  def ap[A, B](ff: F[A => B])(fa: F[A]): F[B]

}


implicit   val   optionApplicative:   Applicative[Option]   =   new
Applicative[Option] {

  def pure[A](a: A): Option[A] = Some(a)


  def ap[A, B](ff: Option[A => B])(fa: Option[A]): Option[B] = (ff,
fa) match {

    case (Some(f), Some(a)) => Some(f(a))

    case _                   => None

  }

}
```

Example in JavaScript

```javascript
const add = x => y => x + y;


const Just = x => ({

  map: f => Just(f(x)),
```

```
  ap: other => other.map(x),

  value: x

});
```

```
const result = Just(add)

  .ap(Just(3))

  .ap(Just(4));
```

```
console.log(result.value); // 7
```

Applicatives allow working with multiple wrapped values at once, making them useful for **parsing, validation, and asynchronous computations**.

Monads: Chaining Computations

A **monad** is an applicative functor that supports **chaining computations**. It is the most powerful of the three structures.

Monad Laws

Left Identity: Wrapping a value and then applying a function should be the same as applying the function directly.
kotlin

```
return x >>= f ≡ f x
```

　　1.

Right Identity: Applying `return` should not change the computation.
kotlin

```
m >>= return ≡ m
```

　　2.

Associativity: Chaining multiple computations should behave consistently.
rust

```
(m >>= f) >>= g ≡ m >>= (\x -> f x >>= g)
```

3.

Example in Haskell

```haskell
class Monad m where

    return :: a -> m a

    (>>=) :: m a -> (a -> m b) -> m b


instance Monad Maybe where

    return = Just

    Nothing >>= _ = Nothing

    Just x >>= f = f x
```

Example in Scala

```scala
trait Monad[F[_]] extends Applicative[F] {

  def flatMap[A, B](fa: F[A])(f: A => F[B]): F[B]

}
```

Example in JavaScript (Promise as a Monad)

```javascript
const fetchData = id =>

  Promise.resolve({ id, name: "Alice" })

    .then(user => Promise.resolve(user.name));
```

```
fetchData(1).then(console.log); // "Alice"
```

Monads allow **sequencing computations** where each step may produce a new computation, making them useful for **I/O operations, error handling, and async workflows**.

Functors vs. Applicatives vs. Monads

Feature	Functor	Applicative	Monad
Mapping	✓ map	✓ map	✓ map
Wrapped Function Application	✗	✓ ap	✓ flatMap
Chaining	✗	✗	✓ flatMap

Monads **extend** applicatives, which **extend** functors.

Conclusion

Functors, applicatives, and monads are **powerful abstractions** that enable expressive and robust functional programming.

- **Functors** allow **mapping** over wrapped values.
- **Applicatives** allow **applying** wrapped functions.
- **Monads** allow **chaining** computations.

By mastering these concepts, developers can write safer, more maintainable, and highly composable functional code.

Monoids and Semigroups in Functional Design

Monoids and semigroups are foundational algebraic structures in functional programming, providing a formalized way to compose operations and work with data structures. They help ensure correctness, enable elegant abstractions, and optimize performance through parallelization.

By understanding these structures, developers can leverage functional techniques for **data aggregation, transformation, and parallel computing**, making their programs more composable and predictable.

Semigroups: The Foundation of Composition

A **semigroup** is a simple algebraic structure with:

1. **A set of values** (e.g., numbers, strings, or other types).
2. **An associative binary operation** (<>) that combines two values.

Associativity

The key property of semigroups is **associativity**:

```
(a <> b) <> c = a <> (b <> c)
```

This means that grouping does not matter when applying the operation.

Example: String Concatenation

String concatenation is a classic example of a semigroup:

```
"Hello " <> "World" <> "!"

-- Equivalent to:

("Hello " <> "World") <> "!"
```

Since <> (concatenation) is associative, it does not matter how we group operations.

Example in Haskell

```
class Semigroup a where
```

```
(<>) :: a -> a -> a
```

```
instance Semigroup String where

    (<>) = (++)
```

This defines a semigroup where <> is simply the string concatenation operator ++.

Example in Scala

```scala
trait Semigroup[A] {

  def combine(x: A, y: A): A

}
```

```scala
implicit val stringSemigroup: Semigroup[String] = (x, y) => x + y
```

Example in JavaScript

```javascript
const semigroupString = {

  concat: (a, b) => a + b

};
```

```javascript
console.log(semigroupString.concat("Hello ", "World!")); // "Hello
World!"
```

Semigroups are useful when **combining collections, building queries, or aggregating logs**.

Monoids: Adding Identity

A **monoid** extends a semigroup by adding an **identity element**:

1. **Closure under an associative binary operation** (`<>`).
2. **An identity element** (`mempty` or `empty`) that does not change values when combined.

Identity Property

```
a <> mempty = mempty <> a = a
```

For example, 0 is the identity for addition, and `" "` is the identity for string concatenation.

Example: Integer Addition

Addition forms a monoid with:

- **Operation:** `+`
- **Identity:** 0

```
instance Monoid Integer where

    mempty = 0

    mappend = (+)
```

Example in Scala

```scala
trait Monoid[A] extends Semigroup[A] {

  def empty: A

}
```

```scala
implicit val intAdditionMonoid: Monoid[Int] = new Monoid[Int] {

  def combine(x: Int, y: Int): Int = x + y
```

```
    def empty: Int = 0

}
```

Example in JavaScript

```javascript
const monoidNumber = {

  concat: (a, b) => a + b,

  empty: 0

};


console.log(monoidNumber.concat(5, 10)); // 15

console.log(monoidNumber.concat(5, monoidNumber.empty)); // 5
```

Monoids are used extensively in **folding, reducing, and accumulating computations**.

Common Monoids in Functional Programming

Type	Operation	Identity Element
Numbers (Sum)	+	0
Numbers (Product)	*	1
Strings	++ (concatenation)	" "

Lists	++ (concatenation)	[ ]
Booleans (AND)	&&	true
Booleans (OR)	`	

Folding with Monoids

Monoids make **folding (reducing) operations** more elegant and efficient.

Summing a List

```
sumList :: [Int] -> Int
sumList = foldr (+) 0
```

Using a monoid:

```
import Data.Monoid

sumList :: [Int] -> Sum Int
sumList = foldr (<>) mempty
```

Example in JavaScript

```
const numbers = [1, 2, 3, 4, 5];
```

```
const sum = numbers.reduce((acc, x) => acc + x, 0);

console.log(sum); // 15
```

Folding is widely used in **aggregation, data processing, and parallel computations**.

Parallelism with Monoids

Monoids enable **parallel and distributed computing** because of their **associativity** and **identity properties**.

Example: Parallel Summation

Given a large list:

```
[1, 2, 3, 4, 5, 6, 7, 8]
```

We can split it:

```
[1, 2, 3, 4] + [5, 6, 7, 8]
```

```
10 + 26 = 36
```

This is **map-reduce**, where intermediate computations are combined efficiently.

Practical Use Cases of Monoids and Semigroups

1. **Logging Systems**
    - Aggregating logs with string concatenation (`Monoid[String]`).
    - Merging JSON logs (`Monoid[Map]`).
2. **Configuration Merging**
    - Combining user-defined configurations with defaults.

3. **Database Queries**
   - ○ Building SQL queries by concatenating filters.
4. **Parallel Computing**
   - ○ Summing data in distributed systems.
5. **Event Sourcing**
   - ○ Reducing event streams into a single application state.

Comparing Semigroups and Monoids

Feature	Semigroup	Monoid
Associative	✓ Required	✓ Required
Identity Element	✗ Not required	✓ Required
Used in	Concatenation, reduction	Folding, parallelism

Implementing Custom Monoids

A **custom monoid** for combining user scores:

```
data Score = Score Int


instance Semigroup Score where

    Score a <> Score b = Score (a + b)


instance Monoid Score where

    mempty = Score 0
```

Using it:

```
totalScore = Score 10 <> Score 20 <> Score 30   -- Score 60
```

Conclusion

Monoids and semigroups are powerful tools for **structuring operations, composing data, and enabling parallel computations**. By understanding these abstractions, developers can **write more concise, modular, and efficient functional programs**. Whether handling logs, processing large datasets, or composing mathematical operations, monoids and semigroups provide an elegant and scalable approach to managing computation.

Category Theory Foundations for Functional Programming

Category theory provides a **mathematical foundation** for structuring and reasoning about programs in functional programming. By abstracting concepts such as composition, identity, and morphisms, category theory helps developers write **modular, composable, and expressive** code.

In functional programming, **functions, types, and transformations** can be viewed as categorical structures. Understanding these foundations allows us to design more **elegant abstractions**, optimize transformations, and ensure correctness.

Basic Concepts of Category Theory

A **category** consists of:

1. **Objects** – Represent types in functional programming (e.g., `Int`, `String`, `List[A]`).
2. **Morphisms (Arrows)** – Represent functions that map one object to another.
3. **Identity Morphism** – Every object has an identity function (`id`) that maps it to itself.
4. **Composition** – If $f: A \to B$ and $g: B \to C$, then there must be a function $g \circ f: A \to C$ (associativity property).

Example in Haskell: Identity Function

```
id :: a -> a
```

```
id x = x
```

Example in JavaScript

```
const id = x => x;

console.log(id(5)); // 5
```

The **identity function** guarantees that a value remains unchanged when mapped over.

Functors as Morphisms Between Categories

A **functor** is a mapping between categories that:

1. **Preserves identity:** F(id) = id
2. **Preserves composition:** F(g ∘ f) = F(g) ∘ F(f)

In functional programming, functors are implemented as **mappable containers** that apply transformations while preserving structure.

Example in Haskell: Functor Instance for Maybe

```
instance Functor Maybe where

    fmap _ Nothing  = Nothing

    fmap f (Just x) = Just (f x)
```

Example in Scala

```
trait Functor[F[_]] {

  def map[A, B](fa: F[A])(f: A => B): F[B]

}
```

```
implicit val optionFunctor: Functor[Option] = new Functor[Option] {

  def map[A, B](fa: Option[A])(f: A => B): Option[B] = fa match {

    case Some(value) => Some(f(value))

    case None        => None

  }

}
```

A functor ensures that transformations are **consistent and composable**.

Monoids and Monoids in Category Theory

A **monoid** is a special kind of category with:

- **A single object** (e.g., a type like `String`).
- **Endomorphisms** (functions from the object to itself).
- **An associative binary operation** (`<>`).
- **An identity element** (`mempty`).

Example: String Concatenation as a Monoid

```
instance Monoid String where

    mempty = " "

    mappend = (++)
```

```
const monoidString = {

  concat: (a, b) => a + b,

  empty: " "
```

```
};
```

Monoids help structure **data aggregation, logging, and parallel reductions**.

Applicatives and Monoidal Functors

An **applicative functor** extends a functor by allowing **functions wrapped in a context** to be applied to wrapped values.

```
class Functor f => Applicative f where

    pure :: a -> f a

    (<*>) :: f (a -> b) -> f a -> f b
```

Example: Applicative in Haskell

```
instance Applicative Maybe where

    pure = Just

    Nothing <*> _ = Nothing

    (Just f) <*> something = fmap f something
```

Applicatives enable **sequential computations without explicit unwrapping**.

Monads: Category of Endofunctors

A **monad** is a functor that allows **chaining of computations**, ensuring that outputs of one computation are passed to the next.

A monad satisfies:

1. **Left Identity:** `return x >>= f ≡ f x`

2. **Right Identity:** m >>= return ≡ m
3. **Associativity:** (m >>= f) >>= g ≡ m >>= (\x -> f x >>= g)

Example: Monad in Haskell

```
instance Monad Maybe where

    return = Just

    Nothing >>= _ = Nothing

    Just x >>= f = f x
```

Example: Monad in JavaScript (Promises as Monads)

```
const fetchData = id =>

  Promise.resolve({ id, name: "Alice" })

    .then(user => Promise.resolve(user.name));


fetchData(1).then(console.log); // "Alice"
```

Monads allow **chaining computations**, such as handling I/O, state, and effects.

Natural Transformations: Transforming Functors

A **natural transformation** converts one functor into another while preserving structure.

If F and G are functors, a natural transformation η satisfies:

$$\eta\_F \circ fmap\_F = fmap\_G \circ \eta\_F$$

Example: Natural Transformation in Haskell

```
toList :: Maybe a -> [a]

toList Nothing  = []

toList (Just x) = [x]
```

This transforms a `Maybe` functor into a `List` functor.

Category Theory in Practical Functional Programming

1. **Error Handling**
   - `Either` monad handles failures without exceptions.
2. **Composability**
   - Combinators like `map`, `flatMap`, `reduce` ensure modular design.
3. **Parallel Processing**
   - Monoids enable **associative operations** for distributed computing.
4. **State Management**
   - The **State Monad** enables **pure state transformations**.

Conclusion

Category theory provides a **solid theoretical foundation** for functional programming. Concepts like **functors, monoids, applicatives, and monads** enable **powerful abstractions, modular code, and predictable behavior**. By understanding these mathematical principles, developers can write **highly composable, correct, and scalable** functional programs.

Chapter 6: Functional Programming in Modern Languages

Functional Programming in JavaScript (ES6+)

JavaScript, while traditionally an imperative and object-oriented language, has increasingly embraced functional programming principles, especially with the advent of ECMAScript 6 (ES6) and later versions. This evolution allows developers to write more expressive, predictable, and maintainable code using functional paradigms. In this section, we will explore the key functional programming features in modern JavaScript, including pure functions, immutability, higher-order functions, function composition, and monads.

Functional Programming Basics in JavaScript

At its core, functional programming in JavaScript involves:

1. **Pure functions**: Functions that produce the same output for the same input and have no side effects.
2. **Immutability**: Avoiding modification of data after creation.
3. **Higher-order functions**: Functions that take other functions as arguments or return them.
4. **Function composition**: Combining smaller functions to build more complex behavior.
5. **Declarative programming**: Writing code that expresses logic without explicitly defining flow control.

Modern JavaScript provides several built-in methods and syntactical improvements to support these concepts.

Pure Functions in JavaScript

A **pure function** has no side effects and returns the same result for the same input. This makes it easier to test and reason about.

```
// Impure function (modifies external variable)

let count = 0;

function increment() {

    count++;

    return count;

}
```

```
// Pure function (depends only on input)

function add(a, b) {

    return a + b;

}
```

Pure functions are the foundation of functional programming as they allow for **referential transparency**, meaning that a function call can be replaced with its output without changing the program's behavior.

Immutability in JavaScript

In functional programming, immutability is crucial to avoid unexpected changes to data structures. JavaScript has several ways to ensure immutability:

```
const user = { name: "Alice", age: 25 };



// Instead of modifying the object, create a new one

const updatedUser = { ...user, age: 26 };



console.log(user); // { name: "Alice", age: 25 }

console.log(updatedUser); // { name: "Alice", age: 26 }
```

Using **spread operators** and methods like map, filter, and reduce help maintain immutability.

Higher-Order Functions

Higher-order functions either take functions as arguments or return them. They allow for greater code reuse and abstraction.

Example: Using map, filter, and reduce

```
const numbers = [1, 2, 3, 4, 5];


// Double each number

const doubled = numbers.map(n => n * 2);

console.log(doubled); // [2, 4, 6, 8, 10]


// Filter even numbers

const evens = numbers.filter(n => n % 2 === 0);

console.log(evens); // [2, 4]


// Sum all numbers

const sum = numbers.reduce((acc, n) => acc + n, 0);

console.log(sum); // 15
```

These higher-order functions replace the need for traditional loops and encourage a **declarative programming** style.

Function Composition

Function composition is a technique where multiple functions are combined to produce a new function.

```
const capitalize = str => str.charAt(0).toUpperCase() + str.slice(1);

const exclaim = str => str + "!";

const repeat = str => str + " " + str;


const compose = (...functions) => value =>
```

```
functions.reduceRight((acc, fn) => fn(acc), value);
```

```
const excitedGreeting = compose(repeat, exclaim, capitalize);
console.log(excitedGreeting("hello")); // "Hello! Hello!"
```

Composition ensures modular and reusable code.

Currying and Partial Application

Currying transforms a function with multiple arguments into a sequence of functions.

```
const multiply = a => b => a * b;
```

```
const double = multiply(2);
console.log(double(5)); // 10
```

Partial application allows pre-setting some arguments while keeping others open.

```
const add = (a, b) => a + b;
const addFive = add.bind(null, 5);
console.log(addFive(10)); // 15
```

These techniques enhance function reuse and clarity.

Handling Side Effects with Functional Approaches

While JavaScript interacts with the DOM, APIs, and databases—leading to unavoidable side effects—functional techniques like **monads** and **functional pipelines** help manage them.

Example using **Promises** (which follow monadic principles):

```
const fetchData = url =>

    fetch(url)

    .then(response => response.json())

    .then(data => console.log(data))

    .catch(error => console.error(error));
```

```
fetchData("https://jsonplaceholder.typicode.com/todos/1");
```

This isolates the side effect (`fetch`) while maintaining a functional style.

Using Functional Libraries: Lodash and Ramda

JavaScript benefits from functional programming libraries like **Lodash** and **Ramda** to enhance functional programming capabilities.

Example using Lodash:

```
const _ = require("lodash");
```

```
const numbers = [1, 2, 3, 4, 5];
const squared = _.map(numbers, n => n * n);
```

```
console.log(squared); // [1, 4, 9, 16, 25]
```

Example using Ramda:

```
const R = require("ramda");
```

```
const add10 = R.add(10);

console.log(add10(5)); // 15



const isEven = n => n % 2 === 0;

const evens = R.filter(isEven, numbers);



console.log(evens); // [2, 4]
```

These libraries provide powerful utilities that align with functional programming paradigms.

Functional Programming in JavaScript Frameworks

Modern JavaScript frameworks like **React** promote functional programming concepts through:

1. **Functional Components** and hooks (useState, useEffect).
2. **Immutability** in state management (Redux, Recoil).
3. **Pure Functions** for UI rendering.

Example: Functional Component in React

```
import React, { useState } from "react";



const Counter = () => {

    const [count, setCount] = useState(0);



    const increment = () => setCount(count + 1);



    return (

        <div>

            <p>Count: {count}</p>
```

```
        <button onClick={increment}>Increment</button>

    </div>

  );

};


export default Counter;
```

React encourages declarative programming and immutability, making functional programming a natural fit.

Conclusion

Functional programming in JavaScript (ES6+) brings clarity, maintainability, and robustness to code. By embracing **pure functions, immutability, higher-order functions, function composition, and declarative paradigms**, developers can write cleaner, more predictable JavaScript applications. With functional libraries like **Lodash and Ramda**, and frameworks like **React**, functional programming is becoming the preferred approach for modern JavaScript development.

Functional Programming in Python

Python, while traditionally an imperative and object-oriented programming language, has strong support for functional programming. With built-in features like **higher-order functions, first-class functions, immutable data structures, and list comprehensions**, Python allows developers to write functional-style code effectively.

This section explores **functional programming in Python**, covering **pure functions, immutability, higher-order functions, function composition, recursion, lazy evaluation, monads, and real-world applications**.

Functional Programming Basics in Python

Python embraces several key functional programming principles:

- **First-class functions**: Functions are treated as variables and can be assigned, passed as arguments, and returned from other functions.
- **Higher-order functions**: Functions that take other functions as arguments or return them.
- **Immutability**: Preferably using immutable types like tuples and namedtuples.
- **List comprehensions and generator expressions**: Compact, functional alternatives to loops.

- **Recursion**: An alternative to iteration.
- **Lazy evaluation**: Using iterators and generators for efficiency.

First-Class Functions in Python

In Python, functions are first-class citizens, meaning they can be stored in variables, passed as arguments, and returned from other functions.

```python
def greet(name):

    return f"Hello, {name}!"



# Assign function to a variable

greeting = greet

print(greeting("Alice"))  # Output: Hello, Alice!



# Passing function as an argument

def execute_function(func, value):

    return func(value)



print(execute_function(greet, "Bob"))  # Output: Hello, Bob!
```

Higher-Order Functions

A **higher-order function** takes a function as an argument or returns a function.

```python
def apply_twice(func, value):

    return func(func(value))



def add_two(n):
```

```
    return n + 2
```

```
print(apply_twice(add_two, 3))   # Output: 7
```

Python's built-in `map()`, `filter()`, and `reduce()` are higher-order functions.

Using `map()`

Applies a function to each element of an iterable.

```
numbers = [1, 2, 3, 4, 5]
squared = list(map(lambda x: x ** 2, numbers))
print(squared)   # Output: [1, 4, 9, 16, 25]
```

Using `filter()`

Filters elements based on a condition.

```
even_numbers = list(filter(lambda x: x % 2 == 0, numbers))
print(even_numbers)   # Output: [2, 4]
```

Using `reduce()`

Reduces an iterable to a single value.

```
from functools import reduce
product = reduce(lambda x, y: x * y, numbers)
print(product)   # Output: 120
```

Immutability in Python

Python encourages **immutable data structures** like tuples and namedtuples.

```
from collections import namedtuple

Person = namedtuple("Person", ["name", "age"])
alice = Person(name="Alice", age=30)

# Creating a new instance instead of modifying the existing one
updated_alice = alice._replace(age=31)

print(alice)          # Output: Person(name='Alice', age=30)
print(updated_alice) # Output: Person(name='Alice', age=31)
```

Using **frozenset** for immutable sets:

```
immutable_set = frozenset([1, 2, 3, 4])
```

Function Composition in Python

Function composition involves combining multiple functions into one.

```
def double(x):
    return x * 2


def increment(x):
```

```
    return x + 1


def compose(f, g):

    return lambda x: f(g(x))


double_then_increment = compose(increment, double)


print(double_then_increment(3))  # Output: 7
```

Recursion in Functional Python

Recursion is commonly used in functional programming instead of loops.

```
def factorial(n):

    if n == 0:

        return 1

    return n * factorial(n - 1)


print(factorial(5))  # Output: 120
```

Using **memoization** to optimize recursion:

```
from functools import lru_cache


@lru_cache(maxsize=None)

def fibonacci(n):
```

```
    if n <= 1:

        return n

    return fibonacci(n - 1) + fibonacci(n - 2)


print(fibonacci(10))  # Output: 55
```

Lazy Evaluation with Generators

Generators allow for **lazy evaluation**, which helps with memory efficiency.

```
def infinite_sequence():

    n = 0

    while True:

        yield n

        n += 1


gen = infinite_sequence()

print(next(gen))  # Output: 0

print(next(gen))  # Output: 1
```

Using generator expressions:

```
squares = (x ** 2 for x in range(10))

print(list(squares))  # Output: [0, 1, 4, 9, 16, 25, 36, 49, 64, 81]
```

Handling Side Effects with Monads

Monads help handle side effects functionally. The `Maybe` monad is commonly used to deal with missing values.

```python
class Maybe:

    def __init__(self, value):

        self.value = value


    def bind(self, func):

        return Maybe(func(self.value)) if self.value is not None else self


    def __str__(self):

        return f"Maybe({self.value})"


# Example Usage

result = Maybe(5).bind(lambda x: x * 2).bind(lambda x: x + 3)

print(result)  # Output: Maybe(13)


result_none = Maybe(None).bind(lambda x: x * 2)

print(result_none)  # Output: Maybe(None)
```

Real-World Applications of Functional Programming in Python

Functional Data Processing with Pandas

```python
import pandas as pd
```

```python
df = pd.DataFrame({'A': [1, 2, 3, 4], 'B': [5, 6, 7, 8]})


# Using apply (higher-order function)

df['C'] = df['A'].apply(lambda x: x * 2)

print(df)
```

Functional API Handling with `requests`

```python
import requests


def fetch_data(url):

    response = requests.get(url)

    return response.json() if response.status_code == 200 else None


data = fetch_data("https://jsonplaceholder.typicode.com/todos/1")

print(data)
```

Conclusion

Python provides extensive support for functional programming through **first-class functions, higher-order functions, immutability, recursion, lazy evaluation, and monads**. While Python is multi-paradigm, integrating functional programming principles enhances **code modularity, readability, and testability**.

By leveraging **map, filter, reduce, decorators, generator expressions, and libraries like Pandas**, developers can write highly efficient functional Python applications.

Functional Programming in Scala

Scala is a powerful programming language that combines object-oriented and functional programming paradigms. It provides extensive support for functional programming concepts such as **pure functions, immutability, higher-order functions, pattern matching, lazy evaluation, monads, and functional data structures**. Scala's type system and concise syntax make it an excellent choice for writing functional programs.

This section explores **functional programming in Scala**, covering key concepts, idiomatic patterns, and real-world applications.

First-Class Functions in Scala

In Scala, functions are first-class citizens, meaning they can be assigned to variables, passed as arguments, and returned from other functions.

```
val add = (a: Int, b: Int) => a + b

println(add(2, 3))  // Output: 5
```

Functions can be assigned to variables and passed around:

```
def greet(name: String): String = s"Hello, $name!"


val greeter: String => String = greet

println(greeter("Alice"))  // Output: Hello, Alice!
```

Higher-Order Functions

Scala supports **higher-order functions**, which take other functions as parameters or return them.

```
def applyTwice(f: Int => Int, x: Int): Int = f(f(x))


val double: Int => Int = _ * 2
```

```
println(applyTwice(double, 3))  // Output: 12
```

Scala provides built-in higher-order functions like **map, filter, and reduce**.

Using `map()`

Applies a function to each element of a collection.

```
val numbers = List(1, 2, 3, 4, 5)

val squared = numbers.map(x => x * x)

println(squared)  // Output: List(1, 4, 9, 16, 25)
```

Using `filter()`

Filters elements based on a condition.

```
val evens = numbers.filter(_ % 2 == 0)

println(evens)  // Output: List(2, 4)
```

Using `reduce()`

Reduces a collection to a single value.

```
val sum = numbers.reduce(_ + _)

println(sum)  // Output: 15
```

Immutability in Scala

Scala encourages **immutability** using `val` and immutable collections.

```scala
val immutableList = List(1, 2, 3)

val updatedList = immutableList :+ 4


println(immutableList)  // Output: List(1, 2, 3)

println(updatedList)    // Output: List(1, 2, 3, 4)
```

Using **case classes** for immutable data structures:

```scala
case class Person(name: String, age: Int)


val alice = Person("Alice", 30)

val updatedAlice = alice.copy(age = 31)


println(alice)          // Output: Person(Alice,30)

println(updatedAlice)   // Output: Person(Alice,31)
```

Function Composition

Function composition allows combining multiple functions into one.

```scala
val increment: Int => Int = _ + 1

val double: Int => Int = _ * 2


val incrementThenDouble = increment.andThen(double)

println(incrementThenDouble(3))  // Output: 8
```

```
val doubleThenIncrement = double.compose(increment)

println(doubleThenIncrement(3))   // Output: 7
```

Currying in Scala

Currying transforms a function that takes multiple parameters into a sequence of functions.

```
def multiply(a: Int)(b: Int): Int = a * b


val double = multiply(2) _

println(double(5))   // Output: 10
```

Recursion in Scala

Scala supports recursion as an alternative to iteration.

```
def factorial(n: Int): Int = {

  if (n == 0) 1

  else n * factorial(n - 1)

}



println(factorial(5))   // Output: 120
```

Using **tail recursion** for optimization:

```
import scala.annotation.tailrec
```

```scala
def factorialTailRec(n: Int): Int = {

  @tailrec

  def loop(acc: Int, n: Int): Int = {

    if (n == 0) acc

    else loop(acc * n, n - 1)

  }

  loop(1, n)

}



println(factorialTailRec(5))   // Output: 120
```

Lazy Evaluation

Scala supports **lazy evaluation** using `lazy val` and **streams**.

```scala
lazy val expensiveComputation: Int = {

  println("Computing...")

  42

}



println("Before access")

println(expensiveComputation)   // Output: Computing... 42

println(expensiveComputation)   // Output: 42
```

Using **LazyList** for infinite sequences:

```scala
val naturals: LazyList[Int] = LazyList.from(1)

println(naturals.take(5).toList)  // Output: List(1, 2, 3, 4, 5)
```

Handling Side Effects with Monads

Scala provides monads like **Option, Either, and Try** to handle side effects.

Using Option

```scala
def safeDivide(a: Int, b: Int): Option[Int] =
  if (b == 0) None else Some(a / b)
```

```scala
println(safeDivide(10, 2))  // Output: Some(5)
println(safeDivide(10, 0))  // Output: None
```

Using Either

```scala
def divide(a: Int, b: Int): Either[String, Int] =
  if (b == 0) Left("Cannot divide by zero")
  else Right(a / b)
```

```scala
println(divide(10, 2))  // Output: Right(5)
println(divide(10, 0))  // Output: Left(Cannot divide by zero)
```

Using Try

```scala
import scala.util.{Try, Success, Failure}
```

```
def parseInt(s: String): Try[Int] = Try(s.toInt)
```

```
println(parseInt("42"))  // Output: Success(42)
```

```
println(parseInt("abc"))                //                    Output:
Failure(java.lang.NumberFormatException)
```

Functional Programming in Scala Frameworks

Functional Collections with Cats

Cats provides advanced functional programming utilities.

```
import cats.implicits._
```

```
val option1: Option[Int] = Some(10)
```

```
val option2: Option[Int] = Some(5)
```

```
val sum = (option1, option2).mapN(_ + _)
```

```
println(sum)  // Output: Some(15)
```

Functional Effects with ZIO

ZIO provides functional effects for side effects management.

```
import zio._
```

```
val program: ZIO[Any, Nothing, Unit] =
```

```
ZIO.succeed(println("Hello, Functional Scala!"))
```

```
Runtime.default.unsafeRun(program)
```

Real-World Applications of Functional Scala

Functional Data Processing with Spark

Apache Spark uses functional programming for distributed data processing.

```
val numbers = sparkContext.parallelize(List(1, 2, 3, 4, 5))
val doubled = numbers.map(_ * 2)
```

```
println(doubled.collect().toList)  // Output: List(2, 4, 6, 8, 10)
```

Functional API Handling with Http4s

Http4s provides purely functional HTTP handling.

```
import org.http4s._
import org.http4s.dsl.io._
```

```
val service = HttpRoutes.of[IO] {
  case GET -> Root / "hello" => Ok("Hello, World!")
}
```

Conclusion

Scala provides **powerful functional programming features**, including **pure functions, immutability, higher-order functions, recursion, lazy evaluation, monads, and functional effects**. It enables writing **concise, expressive, and scalable** code using **Cats, ZIO, Spark, and Http4s**.

By leveraging **functional collections, pattern matching, and immutable data structures**, Scala developers can build robust and maintainable applications. Functional programming in Scala is widely used in **distributed computing, data engineering, and backend development**.

Haskell: The Pure Functional Language

Haskell is a purely functional programming language known for its strong static typing, lazy evaluation, and emphasis on immutability. Unlike multi-paradigm languages like Python or Scala, Haskell enforces a functional approach at its core, making it one of the best languages to explore functional programming principles in depth.

This section explores **Haskell's core functional concepts**, including **pure functions, immutability, higher-order functions, type inference, lazy evaluation, monads, and real-world applications**.

Pure Functions in Haskell

A **pure function** in Haskell has no side effects and always produces the same output for the same input.

```
add :: Int -> Int -> Int
add x y = x + y



main = print (add 3 5)   -- Output: 8
```

Haskell functions **do not allow mutable state**, ensuring referential transparency. This makes it easier to reason about and debug programs.

Immutability in Haskell

In Haskell, **all values are immutable** by default. Once a value is assigned, it cannot be changed.

```
x = 10

y = x + 5   -- x remains 10, and y becomes 15
```

Using **immutable lists**:

```
numbers = [1, 2, 3, 4, 5]

doubled = map (*2) numbers
```

```
main = print doubled   -- Output: [2, 4, 6, 8, 10]
```

Higher-Order Functions

Functions in Haskell can accept other functions as arguments and return them as results.

Using map

Applies a function to each element in a list.

```
square :: Int -> Int

square x = x * x
```

```
squares = map square [1, 2, 3, 4, 5]

main = print squares   -- Output: [1, 4, 9, 16, 25]
```

Using filter

Filters elements based on a condition.

```
evens = filter even [1, 2, 3, 4, 5, 6]
```

```
main = print evens   -- Output: [2, 4, 6]
```

Using `foldr`

Reduces a list to a single value.

```
sumList = foldr (+) 0 [1, 2, 3, 4, 5]
main = print sumList   -- Output: 15
```

Function Composition

Haskell provides function composition using the `.` operator.

```
double :: Int -> Int
double x = x * 2


increment :: Int -> Int
increment x = x + 1


doubleThenIncrement = increment . double
main = print (doubleThenIncrement 3)   -- Output: 7
```

Currying in Haskell

In Haskell, all functions are **curried** by default, meaning they take arguments one at a time.

```
multiply :: Int -> Int -> Int
multiply a b = a * b
```

186 | Functional programming mastery

```
double = multiply 2

main = print (double 5)   -- Output: 10
```

Recursion in Haskell

Since loops are not used in Haskell, **recursion** is the primary way to perform iteration.

Factorial using Recursion

```
factorial :: Int -> Int

factorial 0 = 1

factorial n = n * factorial (n - 1)
```

```
main = print (factorial 5)   -- Output: 120
```

Tail Recursion for Optimization

Using an accumulator to optimize recursion.

```
factorialTail :: Int -> Int -> Int

factorialTail 0 acc = acc

factorialTail n acc = factorialTail (n - 1) (n * acc)
```

```
factorial :: Int -> Int

factorial n = factorialTail n 1
```

```
main = print (factorial 5)   -- Output: 120
```

Lazy Evaluation

Haskell uses **lazy evaluation**, meaning expressions are only computed when needed.

Infinite Lists

```haskell
naturals = [1..]   -- Infinite list
main = print (take 5 naturals)   -- Output: [1, 2, 3, 4, 5]
```

let vs where

Haskell allows defining intermediate computations using let or where.

```haskell
area r = pi * square r
  where square x = x * x


main = print (area 3)   -- Output: 28.27
```

Monads: Handling Side Effects

Monads help manage side effects in a pure functional language like Haskell.

Using Maybe Monad

```haskell
safeDivide :: Int -> Int -> Maybe Int
safeDivide _ 0 = Nothing
safeDivide a b = Just (a `div` b)


main = print (safeDivide 10 2)   -- Output: Just 5
```

Using `Either` Monad for Error Handling

```
safeDivide :: Int -> Int -> Either String Int
safeDivide _ 0 = Left "Cannot divide by zero"
safeDivide a b = Right (a `div` b)
```

```
main = print (safeDivide 10 0)   -- Output: Left "Cannot divide by zero"
```

I/O in Haskell

Haskell uses the `IO` monad for handling input/output operations.

```
main = do
  putStrLn "Enter your name:"
  name <- getLine
  putStrLn ("Hello, " ++ name ++ "!")
```

Real-World Applications of Haskell

Functional Web Development with Yesod

Yesod is a Haskell web framework that enforces type safety.

```
{-# LANGUAGE OverloadedStrings #-}
import Yesod
```

```haskell
data App = App


mkYesod "App" [parseRoutes|

/ HomeR GET

|]


instance Yesod App


getHomeR :: Handler Html

getHomeR = defaultLayout [whamlet| <h1>Hello, Haskell! |]


main :: IO ()

main = warp 3000 App
```

Functional Data Processing with Pandoc

Pandoc, a document converter, is written in Haskell and uses functional principles for data transformation.

```haskell
import Text.Pandoc


convertMarkdown :: String -> Either PandocError Pandoc

convertMarkdown input = runPure $ readMarkdown def input


main = print (convertMarkdown "# Hello, Haskell!")
```

Concurrent Programming with Haskell

Haskell provides **lightweight concurrency** using `forkIO`.

```haskell
import Control.Concurrent

printMessage :: String -> IO ()
printMessage msg = do
  threadDelay 1000000
  putStrLn msg

main = do
  forkIO (printMessage "Hello from thread")
  putStrLn "Main thread running"
  threadDelay 2000000
```

Conclusion

Haskell is a **pure functional language** that enforces **immutability, lazy evaluation, strong static typing, and monads**. It offers concise and expressive syntax for functional programming and is widely used in **web development, data processing, and concurrent programming**.

By leveraging **higher-order functions, recursion, function composition, and type inference**, Haskell developers can write **efficient, safe, and scalable** applications. Its strong mathematical foundation makes it an excellent choice for projects requiring **robust type safety and functional purity**.

Functional Features in Java, C#, and Kotlin

Functional programming has gained significant traction in modern programming languages such as **Java, C#, and Kotlin**, even though they are traditionally object-oriented. Each of these languages has incorporated **functional programming features** like **lambda**

expressions, higher-order functions, immutability, streams, monads, and pattern matching to make code more declarative, concise, and expressive.

This section explores **how Java, C#, and Kotlin implement functional programming** principles and how developers can leverage them to write more maintainable and scalable applications.

Functional Programming in Java

Java introduced functional programming features with **Java 8**, including **lambda expressions, the Stream API, and functional interfaces**. These features have enabled a more functional approach in an otherwise object-oriented language.

Lambda Expressions

Before Java 8, implementing simple functions required creating anonymous classes:

```
import java.util.function.Function;


public class Main {

    public static void main(String[] args) {

        Function<Integer, Integer> square = new Function<Integer,
Integer>() {

            @Override

            public Integer apply(Integer x) {

                return x * x;

            }

        };

        System.out.println(square.apply(5)); // Output: 25

    }

}
```

With **lambda expressions**, the same functionality is written concisely:

```java
import java.util.function.Function;


public class Main {

    public static void main(String[] args) {

        Function<Integer, Integer> square = x -> x * x;

        System.out.println(square.apply(5)); // Output: 25

    }

}
```

Stream API

Java's **Stream API** provides a declarative way to process collections using functional programming.

```java
import java.util.Arrays;

import java.util.List;


public class Main {

    public static void main(String[] args) {

        List<Integer> numbers = Arrays.asList(1, 2, 3, 4, 5);


        numbers.stream()

            .map(x -> x * x)

            .filter(x -> x % 2 == 0)
```

```
            .forEach(System.out::println);   // Output: 4, 16

    }

}
```

Functional Interfaces

Java provides built-in **functional interfaces** like Function, Predicate, and Consumer:

```
import java.util.function.Predicate;


public class Main {

    public static void main(String[] args) {

        Predicate<Integer> isEven = x -> x % 2 == 0;

        System.out.println(isEven.test(4)); // Output: true

    }

}
```

Immutability in Java

Java encourages immutability using **final** and immutable collections.

```
import java.util.Collections;

import java.util.List;


public class Main {

    public static void main(String[] args) {

        List<String> list = List.of("apple", "banana", "cherry");
```

```
        System.out.println(list);

    }

}
```

Functional Programming in C#

C# supports functional programming with **lambda expressions, LINQ, immutable data structures, and functional pipelines**.

Lambda Expressions

C# provides concise lambda expressions for defining functions:

```
using System;


class Program {

    static void Main() {

        Func<int, int> square = x => x * x;

        Console.WriteLine(square(5)); // Output: 25

    }

}
```

LINQ (Language Integrated Query)

LINQ enables declarative querying of collections:

```
using System;

using System.Linq;
```

```
class Program {

    static void Main() {

        var numbers = new[] { 1, 2, 3, 4, 5 };

        var squaredEvens = numbers

            .Select(x => x * x)

            .Where(x => x % 2 == 0);

        foreach (var num in squaredEvens) {

            Console.WriteLine(num);   // Output: 4, 16

        }

    }

}
```

Higher-Order Functions in C#

C# allows passing functions as parameters.

```
using System;

class Program {

    static int ApplyFunction(Func<int, int> func, int value) {

        return func(value);

    }
```

```
static void Main() {

    Func<int, int> increment = x => x + 1;

    Console.WriteLine(ApplyFunction(increment, 5)); // Output: 6

  }

}
```

Immutability in C#

C# supports immutability with **readonly** and **record types**.

```
public record Person(string Name, int Age);


class Program {

    static void Main() {

        var person = new Person("Alice", 30);

        var updatedPerson = person with { Age = 31 };

        Console.WriteLine(updatedPerson); // Output: Person { Name =
Alice, Age = 31 }

    }

}
```

Functional Programming in Kotlin

Kotlin, developed by JetBrains, is a modern language with first-class functional programming support. It provides **higher-order functions, lambda expressions, immutability, and coroutines**.

Lambda Expressions in Kotlin

```kotlin
val square: (Int) -> Int = { x -> x * x }

println(square(5))  // Output: 25
```

Higher-Order Functions

```kotlin
fun applyFunction(f: (Int) -> Int, value: Int): Int {

    return f(value)

}
```

```kotlin
val increment: (Int) -> Int = { x -> x + 1 }

println(applyFunction(increment, 5))  // Output: 6
```

Functional Collections

Kotlin's map, filter, and reduce are commonly used for functional data processing.

```kotlin
val numbers = listOf(1, 2, 3, 4, 5)
```

```kotlin
val squaredEvens = numbers

    .map { it * it }

    .filter { it % 2 == 0 }
```

```kotlin
println(squaredEvens)  // Output: [4, 16]
```

Immutability in Kotlin

Immutable data structures can be created using `val` and `data class`.

```
data class Person(val name: String, val age: Int)

val person = Person("Alice", 30)
val updatedPerson = person.copy(age = 31)

println(updatedPerson)  // Output: Person(name=Alice, age=31)
```

Functional Error Handling with `Result`

Kotlin provides the `Result` type for functional error handling.

```
fun safeDivide(a: Int, b: Int): Result<Int> =
    if (b == 0)  Result.failure(IllegalArgumentException("Cannot
divide by zero"))
    else Result.success(a / b)

println(safeDivide(10, 2))  // Output: Success(5)
println(safeDivide(10,        0))                    //        Output:
Failure(java.lang.IllegalArgumentException: Cannot divide by zero)
```

Coroutines for Functional Concurrency

Kotlin's **coroutines** provide functional, non-blocking concurrency.

```
import kotlinx.coroutines.*
```

```
fun main() = runBlocking {

    launch {

        delay(1000L)

        println("Hello from coroutine!")

    }

    println("Main thread running")

}
```

Conclusion

Java, C#, and Kotlin have embraced **functional programming** to improve code clarity, reduce side effects, and enable declarative programming.

- **Java** provides **Streams, lambda expressions, and functional interfaces**.
- **C#** supports **LINQ, immutable data structures, and higher-order functions**.
- **Kotlin** offers **first-class functional programming features like lambda expressions, higher-order functions, coroutines, and functional error handling**.

By integrating functional programming with object-oriented paradigms, these languages allow developers to write more **concise, testable, and scalable** applications.

Chapter 7: Functional Programming in Real-World Applications

Functional Programming in Web Development

Functional programming (FP) has gained significant traction in web development due to its ability to improve code maintainability, testability, and reliability. Modern web applications often deal with asynchronous data flows, user interactions, and state management—areas where FP provides powerful solutions.

This section explores how FP principles apply to web development, covering topics such as declarative UI design, immutable state management, pure functions in event handling, and functional approaches to data fetching. We also examine FP in popular web frameworks and libraries, showcasing how they leverage functional patterns to create scalable and predictable applications.

Declarative UI Development with Functional Programming

One of the most significant contributions of functional programming to web development is the shift from imperative to declarative UI design. Instead of manually updating the DOM, modern frameworks like React, Solid, and Svelte use a declarative approach where the UI is a function of the application state.

For example, in React, the UI is expressed as pure functions that take state as input and return JSX (JavaScript XML), which represents the desired UI structure.

```
const Greeting = ({ name }) => <h1>Hello, {name}!</h1>;
```

This approach ensures that the UI remains predictable and easy to reason about, as it always reflects the latest application state.

Functional Event Handling

Event handling in web applications is another area where FP principles shine. Instead of modifying global state directly, functional approaches encourage handling events in a pure and composable manner.

Consider a form submission handler in React:

```
const handleSubmit = (event) => {
```

```
event.preventDefault();

const formData = new FormData(event.target);

console.log(Object.fromEntries(formData));
};
```

This function remains pure because it does not mutate any external state. Instead, it extracts the form data and logs it, making it easy to test and reuse.

Immutable State Management

Managing state in web applications can become complex, especially as applications grow in size. Immutable state management, a core FP principle, ensures that state updates do not introduce unintended side effects.

Libraries like Redux and Zustand leverage immutable state updates:

```
const reducer = (state, action) => {

  switch (action.type) {

    case "INCREMENT":

      return { count: state.count + 1 };

    case "DECREMENT":

      return { count: state.count - 1 };

    default:

      return state;

  }
};
```

Since the `reducer` function always returns a new state instead of modifying the existing state, debugging and testing become more manageable.

Functional Data Fetching

Fetching data from APIs is a crucial aspect of web applications. Using pure functions and immutable data structures simplifies data fetching.

For example, using `fetch` with `async/await`:

```
const fetchData = async (url) => {

  const response = await fetch(url);

  return response.json();

};



fetchData("https://api.example.com/data").then(console.log);
```

Since `fetchData` is pure (it only depends on the input `url`), it can be easily tested by mocking the API response.

Streams and Functional Pipelines

Functional streams and pipelines are useful for processing real-time data in web applications. Libraries like RxJS enable functional reactive programming (FRP), allowing developers to handle asynchronous events as data streams.

For instance, processing user input events:

```
import { fromEvent } from "rxjs";

import { map, debounceTime } from "rxjs/operators";



const searchBox = document.getElementById("search");

const searchStream = fromEvent(searchBox, "input").pipe(

  debounceTime(300),

  map(event => event.target.value)

);
```

```
searchStream.subscribe(value => console.log("Search:", value));
```

Here, user input is treated as a stream, and FP techniques like map and debounceTime are used to transform and control event processing.

Functional Routing

Routing in web applications can be implemented functionally by treating routes as pure mappings between URLs and components. Frameworks like Next.js and Remix use file-based routing, while libraries like React Router embrace declarative functional routing:

```
import { BrowserRouter as Router, Route, Routes } from "react-router-dom";

const App = () => (

  <Router>

    <Routes>

      <Route path="/" element={<Home />} />

      <Route path="/about" element={<About />} />

    </Routes>

  </Router>

);
```

This declarative approach makes it easy to reason about route handling, reducing the complexity of navigation logic.

Server-Side Functional Programming

Functional programming is not limited to the frontend. On the backend, FP principles help build scalable and efficient server applications.

For example, in Node.js using Express:

```
const express = require("express");

const app = express();


const requestLogger = (req, res, next) => {

  console.log(`Received request: ${req.method} ${req.url}`);

  next();

};


app.use(requestLogger);

app.get("/", (req, res) => res.send("Hello, Functional World!"));


app.listen(3000, () => console.log("Server running on port 3000"));
```

Here, middleware functions act as pure transformations, making it easy to compose server logic.

Functional Component-Based Frameworks

Modern web frameworks embrace FP principles to improve maintainability and scalability. Some examples include:

- **React**: Functional components and hooks encourage declarative UI development.
- **Elm**: A purely functional language for building web applications.
- **Svelte**: Uses a compiler-based approach to optimize functional state updates.
- **Solid**: A reactive framework with a functional reactivity model.

Conclusion

Functional programming has revolutionized web development by introducing declarative patterns, immutable state management, and pure functions. Whether building UI components, handling events, managing state, or processing data streams, FP principles help create scalable, maintainable, and bug-resistant web applications.

By embracing functional programming in web development, developers can write more predictable, testable, and reusable code, leading to robust applications that stand the test of time.

Functional Programming in Data Science and Machine Learning

Functional programming (FP) has gained significant traction in data science and machine learning due to its ability to handle complex data transformations, ensure immutability, and facilitate parallel computations. Functional paradigms enable data scientists and engineers to write concise, composable, and reusable code, leading to more maintainable and scalable solutions.

This section explores how FP principles enhance data processing, statistical analysis, and machine learning workflows. We discuss functional data transformation, pure functions in feature engineering, lazy evaluation for large datasets, parallel computations with functional approaches, and FP-based machine learning model implementations.

Functional Data Transformation

Data transformation is a crucial step in data science, where raw data is cleaned, processed, and structured for analysis. Functional programming excels in this area by leveraging functions like `map`, `filter`, and `reduce` to perform transformations in a declarative manner.

For example, consider a dataset containing user information:

```
data = [
    {"name": "Alice", "age": 25, "income": 50000},
    {"name": "Bob", "age": 30, "income": 60000},
    {"name": "Charlie", "age": 35, "income": 70000},
]
```

Using `map`, we can extract and transform data functionally:

```
ages = list(map(lambda person: person["age"], data))
```

```
incomes = list(map(lambda person: person["income"] * 1.1, data))  #
Apply a 10% increase
```

```
print(ages)  # [25, 30, 35]
```

```
print(incomes)  # [55000.0, 66000.0, 77000.0]
```

Filtering data is also straightforward:

```
high_earners = list(filter(lambda person: person["income"] > 55000,
data))
```

```
print(high_earners)
```

```
# [{'name': 'Bob', 'age': 30, 'income': 60000}, {'name': 'Charlie',
'age': 35, 'income': 70000}]
```

By using these FP techniques, we ensure that transformations are declarative, side-effect-free, and easily composable.

Pure Functions in Feature Engineering

Feature engineering, the process of creating new features from raw data, benefits significantly from FP. Pure functions ensure that feature transformations remain deterministic and predictable.

For example, scaling numerical features using functional transformations:

```
def normalize(value, min_val, max_val):
    return (value - min_val) / (max_val - min_val)
```

```
ages = [25, 30, 35]
```

```
min_age, max_age = min(ages), max(ages)
```

```
normalized_ages  =  list(map(lambda  age:  normalize(age,  min_age,
max_age),  ages))


print(normalized_ages)  # [0.0, 0.5, 1.0]
```

Here, `normalize` is a pure function that takes an input and produces a predictable output without modifying any global state.

Lazy Evaluation for Large Datasets

Working with large datasets requires efficient computation. Lazy evaluation, a common FP concept, processes data only when needed, reducing memory consumption.

In Python, generators facilitate lazy evaluation:

```
def infinite_sequence():

    num = 0

    while True:

        yield num

        num += 1


sequence = infinite_sequence()

print(next(sequence))  # 0

print(next(sequence))  # 1
```

In data science, tools like `pandas` also support lazy evaluation through `iterrows()` and `apply()`, preventing unnecessary computations.

Parallel and Distributed Computation

Functional programming simplifies parallel and distributed processing by ensuring immutability and stateless computations. Libraries like `multiprocessing` and `dask` in Python leverage FP techniques for efficient parallelism.

Using `multiprocessing` for parallel data processing:

```python
from multiprocessing import Pool


def square(num):
    return num * num


nums = [1, 2, 3, 4, 5]
with Pool() as pool:
    results = pool.map(square, nums)


print(results)  # [1, 4, 9, 16, 25]
```

This approach allows functions to execute concurrently without shared state issues.

Functional Machine Learning Pipelines

Functional programming concepts are widely adopted in machine learning pipelines. Frameworks like TensorFlow, PyTorch, and Scikit-learn provide functional APIs for composing transformations.

Consider a simple Scikit-learn pipeline:

```python
from sklearn.pipeline import Pipeline

from sklearn.preprocessing import StandardScaler

from sklearn.linear_model import LinearRegression
```

```
pipeline = Pipeline([

    ("scaler", StandardScaler()),

    ("model", LinearRegression())

])
```

Each step in the pipeline is a function that transforms the data, ensuring a clean, modular, and reusable workflow.

Functional Approach to Model Training

Training machine learning models functionally involves treating models as pure functions that take data as input and return predictions.

Using a functional approach in PyTorch:

```
import torch

import torch.nn as nn


def create_model():

    return nn.Sequential(

        nn.Linear(2, 10),

        nn.ReLU(),

        nn.Linear(10, 1)

    )


model = create_model()

print(model)
```

Since `create_model` is a pure function, it ensures reproducibility and modularity.

Immutable Data Structures in Data Science

Immutable data structures prevent unintended modifications, a critical feature in large-scale data pipelines. Libraries like PyFunctional provide immutable collections:

```python
from functional import seq


data = seq([1, 2, 3, 4]).map(lambda x: x * 2).filter(lambda x: x > 4).to_list()

print(data)  # [6, 8]
```

Immutable collections help prevent data corruption in complex workflows.

Functional Data Visualization

Data visualization can also benefit from functional programming principles. Libraries like Altair use declarative approaches to create charts:

```python
import altair as alt

import pandas as pd


df = pd.DataFrame({"x": [1, 2, 3], "y": [10, 20, 30]})


chart = alt.Chart(df).mark_line().encode(

    x="x",

    y="y"

)


chart.display()
```

This approach ensures a clean, readable, and functional visualization workflow.

Conclusion

Functional programming significantly enhances data science and machine learning workflows by promoting immutability, composability, and parallel processing. From data transformation and feature engineering to model training and visualization, FP ensures that code remains maintainable, scalable, and efficient.

By leveraging FP techniques, data scientists and engineers can build robust pipelines that efficiently handle large datasets, minimize side effects, and facilitate distributed computations. The adoption of FP in machine learning frameworks further demonstrates its power in creating modular and reproducible models.

Functional Programming in Distributed Systems and Microservices

Functional programming (FP) plays a crucial role in designing distributed systems and microservices by promoting immutability, stateless functions, and high-order composition. These properties make FP well-suited for handling concurrency, fault tolerance, and scalability in large-scale applications.

This section explores how FP principles enhance the design and implementation of distributed systems and microservices. We discuss event-driven architectures, stateless services, function composition for scalability, functional approaches to data consistency, and fault tolerance in distributed environments.

Event-Driven Architecture and Functional Programming

Event-driven architectures (EDA) align well with functional programming because they process events as immutable data structures and use pure functions to handle state transitions.

A common implementation of EDA in FP-based distributed systems is the use of event streams. Consider an example of an event-driven order processing system using Python and `asyncio`:

```
import asyncio

import random
```

```python
async def process_order(order_id):

    print(f"Processing order {order_id}")

    await asyncio.sleep(random.uniform(0.5, 2.0))

    print(f"Order {order_id} completed")


async def main():

    orders = [process_order(i) for i in range(1, 6)]

    await asyncio.gather(*orders)


asyncio.run(main())
```

This system simulates asynchronous event processing where each order is an independent function call, ensuring a non-blocking, scalable system.

Stateless Services for Scalability

A key FP principle is statelessness, which makes microservices more scalable and resilient by avoiding shared mutable state.

Consider a simple stateless microservice in Node.js using Express:

```javascript
const express = require("express");

const app = express();


app.get("/convert/:amount", (req, res) => {

  const amount = parseFloat(req.params.amount);

  const converted = amount * 0.85; // Convert USD to EUR

  res.json({ original: amount, converted });

});
```

```
app.listen(3000,  ()  =>  console.log("Currency  converter  service
running on port 3000"));
```

This service remains stateless as it does not store any user data; each request is processed independently.

Functional Composition for Scalable Services

Functional composition allows distributed systems to be designed as small, composable units rather than monolithic applications. This approach leads to services that can be independently deployed and scaled.

A common technique in FP-based microservices is composing API responses. Consider an example in Python where multiple services fetch user and order data separately and combine the results:

```
import asyncio

import aiohttp


async def fetch_user(user_id):

    async with aiohttp.ClientSession() as session:

        async with session.get(f"http://user-service/{user_id}") as
response:

            return await response.json()


async def fetch_orders(user_id):

    async with aiohttp.ClientSession() as session:

        async with session.get(f"http://order-service/{user_id}") as
response:

            return await response.json()
```

```python
async def fetch_user_data(user_id):

    user, orders = await asyncio.gather(fetch_user(user_id),
fetch_orders(user_id))

    return {**user, "orders": orders}


async def main():

    user_data = await fetch_user_data(1)

    print(user_data)


asyncio.run(main())
```

This functionally composed service allows different microservices to be orchestrated without tight coupling.

Functional Data Consistency in Distributed Systems

One of the challenges of distributed systems is maintaining data consistency. Functional programming helps by enforcing immutability and eventual consistency.

A common approach is using event sourcing, where state changes are captured as immutable events. In a banking system, transactions can be stored as events instead of directly modifying account balances.

Using Python with an immutable ledger:

```python
class Ledger:

    def __init__(self):

        self.transactions = []


    def add_transaction(self, transaction):
```

```
        self.transactions.append(transaction)


    def get_balance(self):

        return sum(t["amount"] for t in self.transactions)


ledger = Ledger()

ledger.add_transaction({"amount": 100, "type": "deposit"})

ledger.add_transaction({"amount": -50, "type": "withdrawal"})


print(ledger.get_balance())   # 50
```

Each transaction is stored as an immutable event, allowing reconstruction of the system state at any time.

Fault Tolerance with Functional Error Handling

Distributed systems must handle failures gracefully. FP provides strong error-handling mechanisms through monadic constructs such as Option, Either, and Try.

Consider an implementation of resilient service calls using Python's asyncio:

```
import asyncio

import random


async def fetch_data():

    if random.random() < 0.3:

        raise Exception("Service unavailable")

    return {"data": "Important result"}
```

```python
async def safe_fetch():

    try:

        return await fetch_data()

    except Exception as e:

        print(f"Error encountered: {e}")

        return {"error": "Fallback response"}


async def main():

    response = await safe_fetch()

    print(response)


asyncio.run(main())
```

Here, failures are handled explicitly, ensuring that the system can continue running even when individual services fail.

Distributed Messaging with Functional Paradigms

Messaging systems like Kafka, RabbitMQ, and NATS leverage functional concepts to process messages in a distributed manner.

Consider a Kafka consumer in Python that processes messages functionally:

```python
from kafka import KafkaConsumer


consumer                    =                    KafkaConsumer("orders",
bootstrap_servers="localhost:9092")
```

```
for message in consumer:

    order = message.value.decode("utf-8")

    print(f"Processing order: {order}")
```

Each message is processed independently, following FP principles of immutability and stateless execution.

Functional Load Balancing and Service Discovery

Load balancing ensures that services distribute workloads evenly across multiple instances. Functional approaches to load balancing use pure functions to determine routing decisions.

A simple round-robin load balancer in Python:

```
class LoadBalancer:

    def __init__(self, services):

        self.services = services

        self.index = 0


    def get_next_service(self):

        service = self.services[self.index]

        self.index = (self.index + 1) % len(self.services)

        return service


services = ["Service A", "Service B", "Service C"]

lb = LoadBalancer(services)


for _ in range(6):

    print(lb.get_next_service())
```

This functionally pure approach ensures fair request distribution.

Immutable Infrastructure with Functional Deployment

Infrastructure-as-code (IaC) tools like Terraform and Pulumi leverage FP concepts to define infrastructure as immutable state.

Example Terraform configuration:

```
resource "aws_instance" "web" {

  ami           = "ami-123456"

  instance_type = "t2.micro"

}
```

Since configurations are immutable, rollback and versioning become straightforward.

Conclusion

Functional programming provides powerful tools for designing scalable, reliable, and maintainable distributed systems and microservices. From event-driven architectures to stateless services, fault tolerance, and load balancing, FP principles ensure that distributed systems remain resilient and efficient.

By leveraging FP techniques, developers can build microservices that are easy to reason about, test, and scale, ensuring that modern distributed applications remain robust in production environments.

Functional Reactive Programming (FRP)

Functional Reactive Programming (FRP) is a programming paradigm that combines functional programming and reactive programming to manage asynchronous data streams declaratively. It is widely used in modern applications, including user interfaces, real-time data processing, and complex event-driven systems.

This section explores the principles of FRP, its advantages over imperative event handling, its implementation in various programming languages, and real-world applications in UI development, data streams, and distributed systems.

Principles of Functional Reactive Programming

FRP is built on the following key principles:

- **Streams as First-Class Entities**: Data changes over time are represented as streams, which can be mapped, filtered, and combined using functional operators.
- **Immutability and Purity**: Transformations on data streams do not mutate state but produce new streams.
- **Declarative Composition**: Complex behaviors are defined through high-level transformations rather than explicit event handling.
- **Asynchronous and Continuous Processing**: Events are continuously processed in response to real-time data updates.

FRP vs. Traditional Event Handling

Traditional event-driven programming relies on imperative callbacks, leading to issues like callback hell and inconsistent state management. FRP addresses these issues by making event handling declarative.

Consider a simple event-driven approach in JavaScript:

```javascript
document.getElementById("button").addEventListener("click", () => {

    console.log("Button clicked!");

});
```

While this works, handling multiple dependent events can quickly become complex. In contrast, FRP treats events as streams, making it easier to manage dependencies and transformations.

Using RxJS, an FRP library in JavaScript:

```javascript
import { fromEvent } from 'rxjs';

import { map } from 'rxjs/operators';


const button = document.getElementById("button");

const clickStream = fromEvent(button, "click").pipe(

    map(() => "Button clicked!")
```

```
);
```

```
clickStream.subscribe(console.log);
```

This approach allows events to be transformed functionally, improving readability and maintainability.

FRP in User Interface Development

FRP is widely used in UI frameworks like React, Elm, and Cycle.js, where the UI is treated as a function of application state.

Consider a React component using the useState and useEffect hooks to handle reactive state updates:

```
import React, { useState, useEffect } from "react";
```

```
const Timer = () => {

    const [count, setCount] = useState(0);


    useEffect(() => {

        const interval = setInterval(() => {

            setCount(prevCount => prevCount + 1);

        }, 1000);


        return () => clearInterval(interval);

    }, []);


    return <h1>Seconds: {count}</h1>;
```

```
};
```

```
export default Timer;
```

This functional approach ensures that state updates occur reactively in response to external events without manual DOM manipulation.

Functional Streams and Data Processing

FRP is commonly used for processing real-time data streams, such as stock prices, sensor data, or live chat messages. Libraries like RxJS in JavaScript and ReactiveX in Python provide functional abstractions for working with streams.

Consider a real-time stock price stream using RxJS:

```
import { interval } from 'rxjs';
import { map } from 'rxjs/operators';


const stockPriceStream = interval(1000).pipe(
    map(() => (Math.random() * 100).toFixed(2))
);
```

```
stockPriceStream.subscribe(price    =>    console.log(`Stock    price:
$${price}`));
```

Each emitted value represents an updated stock price, showcasing how FRP can be used for continuous data processing.

Combining Streams for Complex Behavior

One of the powerful features of FRP is the ability to combine multiple streams into a single transformed stream.

Consider an example where user input and button clicks are combined to create a search functionality:

```
import { fromEvent, combineLatest } from 'rxjs';

import { map } from 'rxjs/operators';


const input = document.getElementById("search");

const button = document.getElementById("submit");


const inputStream = fromEvent(input, "input").pipe(

    map(event => event.target.value)

);


const buttonStream = fromEvent(button, "click");


combineLatest([inputStream, buttonStream]).subscribe(([query]) => {

    console.log(`Searching for: ${query}`);

});
```

Here, changes in the input field and button clicks are combined to trigger a search operation only when both conditions are met.

Reactive State Management

State management in applications can be simplified using FRP. In Redux (a popular state management library in React applications), actions are treated as streams that produce new state objects immutably.

A simple Redux reducer follows functional principles:

```javascript
const reducer = (state = { count: 0 }, action) => {

    switch (action.type) {

        case "INCREMENT":

            return { count: state.count + 1 };

        case "DECREMENT":

            return { count: state.count - 1 };

        default:

            return state;

    }

};
```

Each action transforms the state without modifying it, ensuring predictability.

FRP in Distributed Systems

FRP is also applied in distributed systems, where event-driven architectures require efficient message processing.

Consider an example of an event-driven architecture using Kafka:

```python
from kafka import KafkaConsumer


consumer                    =                    KafkaConsumer("sensor-data",
bootstrap_servers="localhost:9092")


for message in consumer:

    data = message.value.decode("utf-8")

    print(f"Processed sensor data: {data}")
```

Each message is treated as a stream, allowing real-time data ingestion and processing.

Error Handling in FRP

Functional reactive programming provides robust error-handling mechanisms. In RxJS, errors can be caught and transformed into meaningful responses:

```javascript
import { of } from 'rxjs';

import { catchError } from 'rxjs/operators';


const dataStream = of("data").pipe(

    map(() => {

        throw new Error("Something went wrong!");

    }),

    catchError(error => of(`Error handled: ${error.message}`))

);


dataStream.subscribe(console.log);
```

This ensures that failures do not crash the system but are handled gracefully.

Functional Reactive Programming in IoT

In IoT (Internet of Things), devices generate continuous streams of data that need to be processed reactively.

Using RxPy in Python, we can process sensor data:

```python
from rx import interval

from rx.operators import map
```

```
sensor_stream = interval(2).pipe(

    map(lambda _: f"Temperature: {25 + (2 * _)}°C")

)


sensor_stream.subscribe(print)
```

Here, temperature readings are simulated as a reactive stream that updates every two seconds.

Conclusion

Functional Reactive Programming simplifies event-driven programming by treating asynchronous data streams as first-class entities. Whether in UI development, real-time data processing, distributed systems, or IoT applications, FRP ensures code remains declarative, scalable, and maintainable.

By leveraging functional programming principles in FRP, developers can build reactive systems that efficiently handle complex, asynchronous interactions, leading to more responsive and robust applications.

Functional Programming in Game Development

Functional programming (FP) has found a significant role in modern game development due to its emphasis on immutability, pure functions, and declarative programming. These features contribute to improved maintainability, predictable behavior, and efficient parallelism in game development, making FP a valuable paradigm for building complex, interactive, and scalable games.

This section explores how FP principles apply to game development, covering topics such as pure game logic, state management, functional rendering, entity-component-system (ECS) architectures, and reactive programming in game mechanics.

Pure Functions for Game Logic

One of the key advantages of FP in game development is the use of pure functions to define game logic. Pure functions help ensure that the game state is predictable and free from unintended side effects.

Consider a simple game function that calculates the new position of a player based on movement input:

```
def move_player(position, direction):

    movement = {"UP": (0, 1), "DOWN": (0, -1), "LEFT": (-1, 0),
"RIGHT": (1, 0)}

    if direction in movement:

        dx, dy = movement[direction]

        return (position[0] + dx, position[1] + dy)

    return position
```

```
player_position = (5, 5)

new_position = move_player(player_position, "UP")

print(new_position)  # (5, 6)
```

Since `move_player` is a pure function, it does not modify the original state but returns a new state, making it easier to test and debug.

Immutable State Management

Managing game state is one of the most challenging aspects of game development. Functional programming encourages immutability, reducing the risks of unintended modifications and race conditions.

A common approach to state management in functional game development is to use immutable data structures. Consider an immutable game state:

```
from collections import namedtuple
```

```
GameState = namedtuple("GameState", ["player_health", "score"])
```

```
def update_health(state, damage):

    return state._replace(player_health=state.player_health - damage)
```

```
state = GameState(player_health=100, score=0)

new_state = update_health(state, 10)


print(new_state)  # GameState(player_health=90, score=0)
```

By treating game state as immutable, each modification results in a new state, reducing side effects and improving predictability.

Functional Rendering in Games

Rendering is a core part of game development, and FP provides efficient techniques for declaratively describing UI and game visuals.

Consider a functional approach to rendering a simple game scene using Pygame:

```
import pygame


pygame.init()

screen = pygame.display.set_mode((400, 400))


def render(screen, position):

    screen.fill((0, 0, 0))

    pygame.draw.circle(screen, (0, 255, 0), position, 10)

    pygame.display.flip()


position = (200, 200)

running = True

while running:
```

```
    for event in pygame.event.get():

        if event.type == pygame.QUIT:

            running = False

    render(screen, position)



pygame.quit()
```

This functionally structured rendering loop ensures that game visuals remain separate from game logic, leading to a more modular and maintainable architecture.

The Entity-Component-System (ECS) Architecture

The Entity-Component-System (ECS) pattern is a popular architecture in modern game development, leveraging functional principles to manage game objects efficiently.

An ECS-based approach treats game entities as data structures (immutable objects), components as properties, and systems as pure functions that operate on these entities.

A simple ECS model in Python:

```
class Entity:

    def __init__(self, id, components):

        self.id = id

        self.components = components



def move_system(entities):

    for entity in entities:

        if "position" in entity.components and "velocity" in
entity.components:

            pos = entity.components["position"]

            vel = entity.components["velocity"]
```

```
            entity.components["position"] = (pos[0] + vel[0], pos[1]
+ vel[1])

    return entities


# Example entities

player = Entity(1, {"position": (5, 5), "velocity": (1, 0)})

enemy = Entity(2, {"position": (10, 10), "velocity": (-1, 0)})


entities = [player, enemy]

updated_entities = move_system(entities)


for entity in updated_entities:

    print(f"Entity {entity.id}: {entity.components['position']}")
```

This functional approach ensures that systems remain stateless, making it easier to scale and parallelize game logic.

Functional Reactive Programming in Game Mechanics

Games often require real-time handling of user inputs, physics simulations, and AI behaviors. Functional Reactive Programming (FRP) provides a structured way to manage such dynamic game mechanics.

Using RxPy, an FRP library in Python, we can handle continuous player input as a stream:

```
from rx import from_iterable

from rx.operators import map, filter


inputs = ["LEFT", "RIGHT", "UP", "DOWN", "JUMP"]
```

```
input_stream = from_iterable(inputs).pipe(

    filter(lambda x: x != "JUMP"),  # Ignore jump actions

    map(lambda x: f"Processing input: {x}")

)
```

```
input_stream.subscribe(print)
```

By treating inputs as a stream, game logic can be composed in a declarative and scalable manner.

Parallelism and Performance Optimization

Game engines require high-performance computations, often running physics, AI, and rendering in parallel. FP simplifies parallelism by eliminating shared mutable state.

Consider a parallelized function for updating multiple enemy positions using multiprocessing:

```
from multiprocessing import Pool


def update_enemy_position(enemy):

    return (enemy[0] + 1, enemy[1])


enemies = [(10, 10), (15, 20), (5, 5)]

with Pool() as pool:

    updated_enemies = pool.map(update_enemy_position, enemies)


print(updated_enemies)  # [(11, 10), (16, 20), (6, 5)]
```

Using parallel processing, game performance is improved by distributing computations across multiple CPU cores.

Procedural Content Generation with Functional Programming

Procedural Content Generation (PCG) is used in games to create dynamic environments, maps, and characters. FP techniques such as recursion and higher-order functions facilitate PCG.

A simple function to generate a grid-based map procedurally:

```
import random
```

```
def generate_map(width, height):
    return [[random.choice([".", "#"]) for _ in range(width)] for _
in range(height)]
```

```
game_map = generate_map(10, 10)

for row in game_map:

    print("".join(row))
```

By defining content generation as pure functions, games can create infinite, diverse worlds efficiently.

Declarative AI and Behavior Trees

Game AI can benefit from FP by using declarative behavior trees instead of imperative state machines.

A functional approach to AI decision-making using a tree structure:

```
class Node:

    def __init__(self, fn):

        self.fn = fn
```

```
    def execute(self):

        return self.fn()


def attack():

    return "Attacking player"


def patrol():

    return "Patrolling area"


ai_tree = [Node(attack), Node(patrol)]

for node in ai_tree:

    print(node.execute())
```

This declarative AI model allows for composable and reusable behaviors.

Conclusion

Functional programming enhances game development by introducing immutable state management, pure functions for game logic, reactive programming for real-time interactions, and scalable ECS architectures. By leveraging FP principles, game developers can create maintainable, performant, and parallelizable game engines.

From procedural content generation to AI-driven behaviors, FP provides a powerful toolkit for building games that are dynamic, responsive, and scalable. As game development continues to evolve, FP will play an increasingly important role in shaping the future of interactive entertainment.

Chapter 8: Advanced Functional Programming Concepts

Type Systems and Type Inference in Functional Programming

Type systems are fundamental to functional programming, providing a robust way to prevent errors, improve code clarity, and enable compiler optimizations. Strong, static type systems are prevalent in functional languages such as Haskell, Scala, and OCaml, ensuring that many errors are caught at compile-time rather than runtime. This section explores the role of type systems in functional programming, type inference mechanisms, and their impact on software design.

Understanding Type Systems

A **type system** is a set of rules that assigns types to program elements, such as variables, expressions, functions, and modules. It enforces constraints that prevent certain types of runtime errors by checking type correctness at compile-time.

Strong vs. Weak Typing

- **Strongly typed** languages enforce strict type rules, preventing implicit type conversions that may lead to unpredictable behavior. Haskell and Scala are examples of strongly typed languages.
- **Weakly typed** languages allow more implicit conversions, sometimes leading to subtle bugs. JavaScript is often considered weakly typed.

Static vs. Dynamic Typing

- **Statically typed** languages require type annotations or allow inference at compile-time. This prevents type errors before execution.
- **Dynamically typed** languages determine types at runtime, offering flexibility but at the cost of potential runtime errors.

Most functional programming languages favor **strong, static typing** to provide better safety and performance.

Benefits of Type Systems in Functional Programming

- **Error Prevention:** Many common errors (such as null pointer exceptions) are eliminated before runtime.
- **Code Clarity and Maintainability:** Explicit type definitions or inferred types make the code easier to understand and modify.
- **Compiler Optimizations:** The compiler can generate more efficient code when types are known in advance.

- **Better Refactoring:** Strong types make it easier to refactor large codebases without introducing new errors.

Type Inference in Functional Languages

Type inference allows the compiler to determine types automatically without explicit annotations from the programmer. This improves code readability and reduces verbosity while maintaining the benefits of a static type system.

Hindley-Milner Type Inference

Most functional languages, including Haskell and ML, use **Hindley-Milner (HM) type inference**, which enables the compiler to deduce types based on function signatures and usage.

Example in Haskell:

```
add :: Int -> Int -> Int
add x y = x + y
```

With type inference, the compiler can infer the type automatically:

```
add x y = x + y    -- Compiler infers: add :: Num a => a -> a -> a
```

Here, $Num\ a => a -> a -> a$ means the function works for any type a that belongs to the Num type class, making it more generic.

Parametric Polymorphism

Parametric polymorphism allows functions and data structures to be written generically so they work with any type. This is essential in functional programming as it promotes code reuse.

Example in Haskell:

```
identity :: a -> a
identity x = x
```

Here, `identity` works for any type `a`, making it fully generic.

Algebraic Data Types (ADTs)

Functional programming heavily relies on **Algebraic Data Types (ADTs)**, which provide powerful ways to model data structures. The two primary ADTs are:

Product Types (Tuples, Records)

Product types combine multiple values into a single entity.

Example in Haskell:

```
data Point = Point Int Int
```

This `Point` type holds two integers.

Sum Types (Tagged Unions, Variants)

Sum types allow defining values that can be one of several alternatives.

Example in Haskell:

```
data Shape = Circle Float | Rectangle Float Float
```

Here, `Shape` can be either a `Circle` with a radius or a `Rectangle` with width and height.

Type Classes in Functional Programming

A **type class** is a way to define generic operations that can work with multiple types. This is a key feature in Haskell and similar languages.

Example:

```
class Eq a where
  (==) :: a -> a -> Bool
```

Any type that implements `Eq` must provide an implementation for `(==)`. For instance:

```
instance Eq Bool where

  True == True = True

  False == False = True

  _ == _ = False
```

This allows functions to work with any type that supports equality.

Higher-Kinded Types

Higher-kinded types allow the definition of types that operate on other types. This is crucial for working with **monads, functors, and applicatives**.

Example in Haskell:

```
class Functor f where

  fmap :: (a -> b) -> f a -> f b
```

Here, `f` is a type that itself takes another type as an argument (`f a`), such as `Maybe a` or `List a`.

Practical Applications of Type Systems in Functional Programming

1. **Domain Modeling**: Well-defined types improve domain modeling by making invalid states unrepresentable.
2. **Error Handling**: Using types like `Maybe` or `Either` to handle errors rather than relying on exceptions.
3. **Concurrency Safety**: Type systems help enforce immutability, making concurrent programming safer.
4. **Automatic Documentation**: Well-designed type signatures serve as self-documenting code.

Comparison of Type Systems in Functional Languages

Feature	Haskell	Scala	OCaml	Elm
Type Inference	Yes	Yes	Yes	Yes
Strong Typing	Yes	Yes	Yes	Yes
Algebraic Data Types	Yes	Yes	Yes	Yes
Type Classes	Yes	Partial	No	No
Parametric Polymorphism	Yes	Yes	Yes	Yes

Challenges of Strong Static Typing

- **Learning Curve**: Developers unfamiliar with static typing may find it difficult at first.
- **Boilerplate Code**: Some type systems require verbose type definitions.
- **Error Messages**: Type inference can sometimes produce complex error messages that are hard to understand.

Conclusion

Type systems and type inference are foundational to functional programming, providing safety, clarity, and efficiency. While strong static typing has a learning curve, the benefits outweigh the initial complexity, making functional programming a powerful paradigm for writing reliable and maintainable code.

By leveraging type inference, parametric polymorphism, and algebraic data types, functional programmers can write expressive, concise, and error-free code. As functional programming continues to evolve, type systems will remain a crucial part of building scalable and robust software solutions.

Advanced Pattern Matching Techniques

Pattern matching is a powerful feature in functional programming that enables concise, readable, and expressive code. It allows developers to destructure data structures, handle different cases efficiently, and enforce exhaustive checks to prevent unexpected runtime errors. This section explores advanced pattern matching techniques, covering various applications, optimizations, and best practices.

The Basics of Pattern Matching

Pattern matching is commonly used in functional languages like Haskell, Scala, OCaml, and F#. It allows matching values against predefined patterns and executing corresponding code blocks. This replaces verbose conditional statements with more declarative, structured code.

A simple pattern matching example in Haskell:

```
matchNumber :: Int -> String

matchNumber 1 = "One"

matchNumber 2 = "Two"

matchNumber _ = "Other number"
```

This function takes an integer and returns a string representation. The underscore (_) acts as a **wildcard**, matching any value not explicitly defined.

In Scala:

```
def matchNumber(n: Int): String = n match {

  case 1 => "One"

  case 2 => "Two"

  case _ => "Other number"

}
```

Both implementations achieve the same goal using pattern matching rather than imperative conditional statements.

Destructuring in Pattern Matching

Destructuring allows extracting values from data structures during pattern matching. This is particularly useful for handling tuples, lists, and custom data types.

Tuples and Lists

Pattern matching on tuples:

```
describePair :: (Int, Int) -> String

describePair (1, _) = "First is one"

describePair (_, 2) = "Second is two"

describePair _ = "Different pair"
```

Pattern matching on lists:

```
listInfo :: [Int] -> String

listInfo [] = "Empty list"

listInfo [x] = "Single-element list"

listInfo (x:y:_) = "Multiple-element list"
```

This function distinguishes between empty lists, single-element lists, and lists with two or more elements.

Recursive Pattern Matching

Pattern matching works seamlessly with recursion, allowing for elegant solutions to problems that involve iteration.

Example: Summing a list in Haskell:

```
sumList :: [Int] -> Int

sumList [] = 0

sumList (x:xs) = x + sumList xs
```

Here, `x:xs` splits the list into its head (`x`) and tail (`xs`), allowing the function to recursively process the remaining elements.

In Scala:

```scala
def sumList(lst: List[Int]): Int = lst match {

  case Nil => 0

  case x :: xs => x + sumList(xs)

}
```

This recursive approach eliminates the need for explicit loops.

Pattern Matching with Custom Data Types

Functional programming often uses **Algebraic Data Types (ADTs)**, such as **sum types** (variants) and **product types** (records), which are naturally suited for pattern matching.

Sum Types (Variants)

Haskell example:

```haskell
data Shape = Circle Float | Rectangle Float Float


area :: Shape -> Float
area (Circle r) = pi * r * r
area (Rectangle w h) = w * h
```

Here, the `Shape` type can be either a `Circle` with a radius or a `Rectangle` with width and height. Pattern matching enables extracting values directly.

Scala equivalent:

```
sealed trait Shape

case class Circle(radius: Double) extends Shape

case class Rectangle(width: Double, height: Double) extends Shape


def area(shape: Shape): Double = shape match {

  case Circle(r) => Math.PI * r * r

  case Rectangle(w, h) => w * h

}
```

The `sealed trait` ensures that all possible cases are known at compile time, enabling exhaustive pattern checking.

Product Types (Records)

Pattern matching on records:

```
data Person = Person { name :: String, age :: Int }


greet :: Person -> String

greet (Person n a) = "Hello, " ++ n ++ "! You are " ++ show a ++ "
years old."
```

This approach makes extracting fields cleaner compared to traditional accessor functions.

Nested Pattern Matching

Pattern matching can be **nested**, allowing deeper extraction of values.

Example in Haskell:

```
data Tree a = Leaf a | Node (Tree a) (Tree a)


depth :: Tree a -> Int

depth (Leaf _) = 1

depth (Node left right) = 1 + max (depth left) (depth right)
```

In this example, pattern matching is used recursively to determine the depth of a binary tree.

Scala equivalent:

```
sealed trait Tree[+A]

case class Leaf[A](value: A) extends Tree[A]

case class Node[A](left: Tree[A], right: Tree[A]) extends Tree[A]


def depth[A](tree: Tree[A]): Int = tree match {

  case Leaf(_) => 1

  case Node(left, right) => 1 + (depth(left) max depth(right))

}
```

Nested pattern matching provides elegant solutions for tree traversal problems.

Guards in Pattern Matching

Guards extend pattern matching by allowing **conditional checks**.

Example in Haskell:

```haskell
describeAge :: Int -> String

describeAge age
  | age < 13 = "Child"
  | age < 20 = "Teenager"
  | otherwise = "Adult"
```

Scala equivalent:

```scala
def describeAge(age: Int): String = age match {
  case a if a < 13 => "Child"
  case a if a < 20 => "Teenager"
  case _ => "Adult"
}
```

Guards enhance flexibility by adding constraints within patterns.

Exhaustiveness Checking and Compiler Safety

Many functional languages enforce **exhaustive pattern matching**, ensuring all possible cases are handled.

Example in Haskell:

```haskell
data Status = Success | Failure

handleStatus :: Status -> String
handleStatus Success = "Operation succeeded"
```

```
handleStatus Failure = "Operation failed"
```

If a case is omitted, the compiler generates an error, preventing runtime crashes due to unhandled cases.

Scala enforces this using sealed traits:

```
sealed trait Status

case object Success extends Status

case object Failure extends Status


def handleStatus(status: Status): String = status match {

  case Success => "Operation succeeded"

  case Failure => "Operation failed"

}
```

This ensures all cases are covered.

Optimizing Pattern Matching Performance

Although pattern matching is efficient, improper use can lead to performance issues. Here are some optimization techniques:

1. **Use Ordered Matching:** Place the most frequently matched cases first.
2. **Avoid Deep Nesting:** Excessive nesting can impact readability and performance.
3. **Leverage Compiler Optimizations:** Functional languages often optimize pattern matching internally.
4. **Prefer Sealed Traits:** In Scala, using sealed ensures exhaustive matching and better optimizations.

Example of avoiding redundant checks:

```
isEven :: Int -> Bool

isEven n

  | n `mod` 2 == 0 = True

  | otherwise = False
```

This is more efficient than a full match case.

Conclusion

Advanced pattern matching techniques enhance the expressiveness, safety, and efficiency of functional programming. By leveraging destructuring, recursion, custom data types, guards, and exhaustive matching, developers can write concise and maintainable code.

Pattern matching is a core feature of functional programming languages, making them well-suited for complex data transformations and domain modeling. Mastering these techniques enables developers to write robust, readable, and efficient programs, reducing errors while improving maintainability.

Purely Functional State Management

State management is one of the key challenges in software development, especially in large-scale applications. Traditional state management approaches often rely on mutable state, which can lead to unintended side effects, race conditions, and difficult-to-debug errors. Functional programming, by contrast, promotes **purely functional state management**, where state changes are modeled using immutable data structures and pure functions. This ensures greater predictability, testability, and composability.

This section explores key concepts, techniques, and real-world implementations of purely functional state management.

The Challenge of State in Functional Programming

In imperative programming, state is often stored in mutable variables that change over time. This approach introduces several issues:

- **Unpredictability**: Mutations make it harder to track how and when the state changes.
- **Concurrency Issues**: Mutable state can lead to race conditions in multi-threaded applications.
- **Difficulty in Debugging**: Unexpected state changes make debugging complex.

Functional programming addresses these issues by treating state updates as a series of immutable transformations rather than direct mutations.

Example of mutable state in an imperative language:

```
counter = 0


def increment():

    global counter

    counter += 1
```

In this approach, counter is mutable, making the function impure.

A purely functional alternative in Haskell:

```
increment :: Int -> Int
increment count = count + 1
```

Here, increment is a pure function that does not mutate any external state. Instead, it takes an argument and returns a new value.

Immutable State and Persistent Data Structures

Functional state management relies on **immutable state**, where every state change produces a new version of the state instead of modifying the existing one.

Example: Managing a Counter with Immutable State

In JavaScript using a functional approach:

```
const increment = (count) => count + 1;
```

```
let state = 0;

state = increment(state);

console.log(state); // 1
```

Since `increment` does not modify the existing state, the function remains pure.

Many functional programming languages provide **persistent data structures**, which enable efficient state management by reusing parts of previous states instead of creating deep copies.

Example in Clojure:

```
(def counter 0)


(defn increment [count] (+ count 1))


(def new-counter (increment counter))
```

Clojure's data structures are **persistent**, meaning previous versions of `counter` remain accessible even after updates.

State Management Using Monads

In purely functional languages like Haskell, state is often modeled using **monads**. The `State` monad provides a structured way to handle state transformations while keeping functions pure.

Defining a Simple State Monad in Haskell

```
import Control.Monad.State


type CounterState = State Int
```

```
increment :: CounterState ()

increment = modify (+1)
                     •


runState increment 0   -- ((),1)
```

Here:

- `State Int` represents a stateful computation where `Int` is the state.
- `modify (+1)` updates the state without mutating it.
- `runState increment 0` executes the state transformation, returning a new state.

This ensures state changes are encapsulated in a controlled manner, preserving purity.

Functional State Management in Real-World Applications

Many functional programming languages and frameworks provide state management tools based on immutable state and pure transformations.

State Management in Redux (JavaScript/TypeScript)

Redux is a widely used functional state management library in JavaScript applications. It enforces **unidirectional data flow** and uses **pure reducers** to update state.

Example:

```
const initialState = { count: 0 };


const reducer = (state = initialState, action) => {

  switch (action.type) {

    case "INCREMENT":

      return { ...state, count: state.count + 1 };

    case "DECREMENT":
```

```
      return { ...state, count: state.count - 1 };

    default:

      return state;

  }

};
```

```
console.log(reducer(initialState, { type: "INCREMENT" })); // { count:
1 }
```

Key aspects:

- **Reducers are pure functions**: They take `state` and `action` as input and return a new state.
- **State is immutable**: Every update creates a new state object.

Elm: A Purely Functional State Model

Elm, a functional programming language for front-end development, enforces a strictly functional approach to state management using the **Model-Update-View (MVU) pattern**.

Example of an Elm update function:

```
type Msg = Increment | Decrement

update : Msg -> Model -> Model

update msg model =

    case msg of

        Increment -> { model | count = model.count + 1 }

        Decrement -> { model | count = model.count - 1 }
```

Elm enforces immutability and pure state transformations, making debugging easier.

Managing Complex State with Lenses

When working with deeply nested immutable state, updating specific fields can be cumbersome. **Lenses** provide a composable way to update immutable structures without unnecessary boilerplate.

Example in Haskell using `lens`:

```
import Control.Lens

data User = User { _name :: String, _age :: Int } deriving (Show)
makeLenses ''User

updateAge :: User -> User
updateAge = over age (+1)
```

Lenses allow updating nested fields without mutating the original structure.

Event Sourcing and Functional State Management

Event sourcing is a functional approach to state management where **state is derived from a sequence of events** rather than being stored directly. This technique is used in distributed systems and domain-driven design.

Basic Event Sourcing Example in Scala

```
sealed trait Event

case class Incremented(amount: Int) extends Event

case class Decremented(amount: Int) extends Event
```

```
def applyEvent(state: Int, event: Event): Int = event match {

  case Incremented(amount) => state + amount

  case Decremented(amount) => state - amount

}
```

With event sourcing:

- **State is immutable**: Each event describes a transformation.
- **Historical events can be replayed** to reconstruct state.

Concurrency in Functional State Management

In multi-threaded applications, managing shared state without race conditions is critical. Functional programming achieves **safe concurrency** through:

1. **Immutable data**: Since state never changes, concurrent access is safe.
2. **Software Transactional Memory (STM)**: Used in Haskell to handle concurrent state updates.
3. **Actors and Message Passing**: Used in functional languages like Erlang and Scala.

Example: Using STM in Haskell

```
import Control.Concurrent.STM


main = do

    counter <- newTVarIO 0

    atomically $ modifyTVar' counter (+1)
```

STM ensures atomic updates without locks, making concurrent state management safer.

Comparing Functional and Imperative State Management

Feature	Functional Approach	Imperative Approach
State Mutability	Immutable state	Mutable state
Concurrency Safety	High (no race conditions)	Low (requires locks)
Debugging	Easier (pure functions)	Harder (hidden state changes)
Predictability	High (no side effects)	Low (state changes unpredictably)
Scalability	More scalable	Less scalable

Functional state management results in **more reliable, maintainable, and scalable** applications.

Conclusion

Purely functional state management eliminates many pitfalls of mutable state, offering **predictability, concurrency safety, and maintainability**. Techniques such as **immutable state, persistent data structures, monads, lenses, event sourcing, and STM** provide robust solutions for managing state functionally.

While adopting functional state management requires a paradigm shift, the benefits far outweigh the initial learning curve. From **simple counter updates to complex concurrent systems**, functional programming offers a structured and scalable way to manage state in modern applications.

Domain-Specific Languages (DSLs) in Functional Programming

Domain-Specific Languages (DSLs) are specialized programming languages or notations tailored to a specific problem domain. Unlike general-purpose languages (GPLs) such as Haskell, Scala, or Python, DSLs are designed to express domain logic concisely and efficiently. Functional programming provides powerful abstractions for constructing DSLs due to its strong emphasis on **composability, immutability, and declarative syntax**.

This section explores **internal and external DSLs, compositional design, embedded DSLs,** and **real-world applications** of DSLs in functional programming.

What is a Domain-Specific Language (DSL)?

A **DSL** is a language designed to solve problems within a **specific domain** rather than being general-purpose. Examples include:

- **SQL** (for database queries)
- **Regex** (for text pattern matching)
- **CSS** (for styling web pages)
- **GraphQL** (for API queries)

DSLs improve **expressiveness**, **safety**, and **readability** by reducing boilerplate and enabling domain experts to interact with complex systems more easily.

Types of DSLs

DSLs are broadly classified into:

1. **Internal DSLs (Embedded DSLs)**
   - Built within an existing general-purpose language.
   - Leverages host language features.
   - Examples: LINQ in C#, Scalaz in Scala.
2. **External DSLs**
   - Implemented as a separate language with its own syntax and parser.
   - Often requires dedicated interpreters or compilers.
   - Examples: SQL, JSON, HTML.

Functional programming is well-suited for **internal DSLs** due to its composability, higher-order functions, and algebraic data types.

Building an Internal DSL in Haskell

Haskell provides rich abstractions for defining internal DSLs using **higher-order functions, algebraic data types, and monads**.

Example: A Simple Arithmetic DSL

```
data Expr
```

```
= Lit Int

| Add Expr Expr

| Mul Expr Expr


eval :: Expr -> Int

eval (Lit n) = n

eval (Add x y) = eval x + eval y

eval (Mul x y) = eval x * eval y


expr1 = Add (Lit 2) (Mul (Lit 3) (Lit 4)) -- Represents 2 + (3 * 4)

main = print (eval expr1)   -- Output: 14
```

This DSL allows defining mathematical expressions declaratively. The `eval` function interprets the expressions.

Compositional DSL Design

One of the advantages of functional DSLs is **composability**, allowing small, reusable components to build complex expressions.

Example: A Financial DSL in Haskell

```
data Trade = Buy String Int | Sell String Int


portfolio :: [Trade]

portfolio = [Buy "AAPL" 100, Sell "GOOGL" 50, Buy "MSFT" 75]


describe :: Trade -> String
```

```
describe (Buy stock qty) = "Buy " ++ show qty ++ " shares of " ++
stock

describe (Sell stock qty) = "Sell " ++ show qty ++ " shares of " ++
stock


main = mapM_ (putStrLn . describe) portfolio
```

This DSL enables declarative trade specifications.

Monads and DSLs

Monads provide a structured way to model computation in DSLs.

Example: A Logging DSL Using Monads in Haskell

```
import Control.Monad.Writer


logAction :: String -> Writer [String] ()

logAction msg = tell [msg]


workflow :: Writer [String] ()

workflow = do

    logAction "Starting process"

    logAction "Processing data"

    logAction "Finishing process"


main = mapM_ putStrLn (execWriter workflow)
```

The `Writer` monad allows capturing logs **without explicit state mutation**, improving **composability and readability**.

Building an External DSL

External DSLs require **parsing and interpretation**. Many functional languages provide parsing libraries.

Example: A JSON DSL Parser in Haskell

```haskell
import Data.Aeson

import qualified Data.ByteString.Lazy as B


data User = User { name :: String, age :: Int } deriving Show


instance FromJSON User where

  parseJSON = withObject "User" $ \v -> User

    <$> v .: "name"

    <*> v .: "age"


main = do

  jsonData <- B.readFile "user.json"

  let user = decode jsonData :: Maybe User

  print user
```

This external DSL processes JSON data using **Aeson** in Haskell.

Real-World Applications of DSLs in Functional Programming

1. **Configuration Management**
   - DSLs like **Nix** (Haskell-based) manage system configurations declaratively.
2. **Infrastructure as Code (IaC)**
   - **Terraform** and **Pulumi** use DSLs to define cloud infrastructure.
3. **Machine Learning and Data Science**
   - TensorFlow provides a Python-based DSL for defining computational graphs.
4. **Build Systems**
   - **Makefiles** and **Bazel** use DSLs for dependency management.
5. **Game Development**
   - Functional DSLs model game logic using composable rules.

DSLs and Type Safety

Functional programming ensures **type safety in DSLs**, reducing runtime errors.

Example: A Type-Safe Units DSL in Haskell

```
data Unit = Meter | Second | Kilogram

data Measurement = Measurement Double Unit


addMeasure :: Measurement -> Measurement -> Maybe Measurement

addMeasure (Measurement v1 u1) (Measurement v2 u2)

  | u1 == u2  = Just (Measurement (v1 + v2) u1)

  | otherwise = Nothing  -- Prevents invalid operations
```

This prevents **invalid operations** like adding meters to seconds.

Comparing DSLs to General-Purpose Languages

Feature	General-Purpose Language	Domain-Specific Language

Expressiveness	High, but verbose	Concise and focused
Performance	Optimized for general use	Optimized for domain-specific tasks
Ease of Use	Requires learning language syntax	Easier for domain experts
Type Safety	Varies by language	Often enforced via design

DSLs improve **code clarity and maintainability** in specialized domains.

Challenges of DSLs

Despite their advantages, DSLs have challenges:

- **Design Complexity**: Crafting an effective DSL requires deep domain knowledge.
- **Learning Curve**: Users must understand DSL semantics.
- **Performance Overhead**: Some DSLs add abstraction overhead.
- **Integration**: External DSLs require parsers and interpreters.

Well-designed DSLs **balance expressiveness and simplicity**.

Conclusion

Domain-Specific Languages (DSLs) are a powerful abstraction in functional programming, enabling expressive, **declarative**, and **type-safe** solutions for specialized problems. By leveraging **higher-order functions, monads, algebraic data types, and composability**, functional languages like **Haskell, Scala, and Clojure** provide a robust foundation for DSL development.

From **internal DSLs like Redux** to **external DSLs like SQL**, the use of functional paradigms ensures **maintainability, reliability, and conciseness**. While designing DSLs presents challenges, their benefits in **code clarity, safety, and efficiency** make them indispensable for solving domain-specific problems.

Mastering DSLs in functional programming opens up new possibilities in **infrastructure automation, data processing, machine learning, and beyond**, allowing developers to build expressive and scalable domain-oriented solutions.

Meta-Programming and Functional Code Generation

Meta-programming is a programming technique where code is treated as data, enabling programs to **generate, modify, and manipulate** code at runtime or compile time. Functional programming provides **powerful abstractions** for meta-programming through **higher-order functions, macros, code transformation, and lazy evaluation**.

This section explores **meta-programming concepts, functional techniques for code generation**, and **real-world applications in functional programming**.

Understanding Meta-Programming

Meta-programming enables **dynamic and compile-time code manipulation**, reducing boilerplate and improving maintainability. It is commonly used for:

- **Code Generation**: Automatically generating repetitive code.
- **Reflection**: Inspecting and modifying program structures at runtime.
- **Macros and Compile-Time Evaluation**: Executing code transformations at compilation.

Examples of meta-programming in different paradigms:

- **Macros in Lisp**
  - Lisp macros generate new syntax constructs at compile time.
- **Template Metaprogramming in C++**
  - C++ uses templates for compile-time computation.
- **Reflection in Java and C#**
  - These languages inspect types and modify objects dynamically.

Functional programming takes a **declarative** approach to meta-programming, leveraging **immutability and composability** for safer and more predictable transformations.

Functional Approaches to Meta-Programming

Functional languages provide **higher-order functions, lazy evaluation, macros, and type systems** for meta-programming.

Key techniques include:

1. **Code as Data (Homoiconicity)**
   - Treating code as data structures that can be manipulated programmatically.
2. **Lazy Evaluation and Symbolic Computation**
   - Delaying computation until needed, enabling **on-demand code transformation**.
3. **Macros and Template Expansion**

       ○ Using **compile-time code generation** to reduce runtime overhead.
4. **Type-Level Computation**
       ○ Leveraging **type inference and algebraic data types** for safe, generic meta-programming.

Code as Data: The Foundation of Meta-Programming

Homoiconicity refers to languages where **code is represented as a data structure**, allowing programs to modify themselves. Lisp-based languages like Clojure and Scheme are famous for this.

Example: Lisp Macros for Code Generation

```
(defmacro unless [condition then-part else-part]

  `(if (not ~condition) ~then-part ~else-part))
```

```
(unless false (println "Executed") (println "Skipped"))
```

Here:

- `unless` is a **macro** that generates an `if` statement at compile-time.
- The backtick (`\``) and `~` symbols allow **templating**.

Macros **extend the language itself**, enabling **custom syntax**.

Lazy Evaluation for On-Demand Code Generation

Lazy evaluation defers computation **until a value is needed**, making it useful for **symbolic computation and infinite data structures**.

Example: Infinite Data Structures in Haskell

```
lazyList :: [Int]

lazyList = [1..]   -- Infinite list
```

```
take 10 lazyList  -- Extracts first 10 elements without computing the
rest
```

By **delaying execution**, functional languages optimize **performance and memory usage**.

Macros in Functional Programming

Macros allow **compile-time code transformations**, eliminating runtime overhead.

Example: Scala Macros

```
import scala.language.experimental.macros

import scala.reflect.macros.blackbox.Context


object MacroExample {

  def log(msg: String): Unit = macro logImpl


  def logImpl(c: Context)(msg: c.Expr[String]): c.Expr[Unit] = {

    import c.universe._

    reify { println("LOG: " + msg.splice) }

  }

}
```

Here:

- `log` generates a compile-time **logging function**.
- `reify` enables **AST (Abstract Syntax Tree) transformations**.

Macros in functional languages ensure **type safety** while optimizing performance.

Type-Level Computation and Generics

Functional programming enables **type-driven code generation**, ensuring correctness at compile-time.

Example: Type-Level Programming in Haskell

```
{-# LANGUAGE DataKinds, KindSignatures #-}


data Nat = Zero | Succ Nat


type family Add (a :: Nat) (b :: Nat) :: Nat where

  Add Zero b = b

  Add (Succ a) b = Succ (Add a b)
```

Here:

- `Nat` represents natural numbers at **type level**.
- `Add` performs **compile-time arithmetic**, reducing runtime overhead.

This technique is used in **dependently typed languages** like Idris for **mathematically provable programs**.

Generating Code with Template Haskell

Template Haskell provides **meta-programming facilities** by allowing **compile-time code generation**.

Example: Code Generation with Template Haskell

```
{-# LANGUAGE TemplateHaskell #-}
```

```
import Language.Haskell.TH
```

```
genFun :: Name -> Q [Dec]
genFun name = [d| $(varP name) = "Generated Function" |]
```

```
$(genFun 'generatedFunction)
```

```
main = print generatedFunction   -- Output: "Generated Function"
```

Template Haskell allows **dynamic function creation at compile-time**, reducing boilerplate.

Using Quasi-Quoting for Domain-Specific Languages

Quasi-quoting simplifies **DSL integration** by allowing **inline meta-programming**.

Example: SQL DSL in Haskell

```
{-# LANGUAGE QuasiQuotes #-}
```

```
import Database.PostgreSQL.Simple.SqlQQ
```

```
query = [sql| SELECT * FROM users WHERE age > 30 |]
```

This enables **safer database queries** using **compile-time validation**.

Real-World Applications of Meta-Programming in Functional Programming

Meta-programming has **diverse real-world applications,** including:

1. **DSLs for Code Generation**
   - Used in **ORMs (Object-Relational Mappers)** to generate database queries dynamically.
   - **Example:** LINQ in C#.
2. **Compiler Optimization and Code Transformation**
   - Used in **LLVM-based functional compilers** to generate efficient machine code.
3. **Auto-Deriving Boilerplate Code**
   - Functional languages use meta-programming to generate **serialization, comparison, and equality checks**.
   - **Example:** Deriving Eq and Show in Haskell.
4. **Type-Level Guarantees in Critical Systems**
   - Used in **dependently typed languages** to prevent errors **before runtime**.
   - **Example:** Type-driven theorem provers in Agda and Idris.
5. **Optimized Functional Reactive Programming (FRP)**
   - Meta-programming is used to optimize **stream transformations** in reactive systems.
   - **Example:** Reflex FRP in Haskell.

Comparing Meta-Programming Techniques

Technique	Compile-Time?	Runtime Overhead	Safety
Macros	Yes	None	High
Lazy Evaluation	No	Low	Medium
Type-Level Computation	Yes	None	High
Quasi-Quoting	Yes	Low	High

Each approach **balances flexibility and performance**, depending on the use case.

Challenges of Meta-Programming

Despite its power, meta-programming comes with challenges:

- **Complexity**: Requires deep understanding of **AST transformations**.
- **Debugging Difficulty**: Errors in generated code can be hard to trace.
- **Compile-Time Overhead**: Extensive meta-programming increases **compilation time**.
- **Security Risks**: Dynamic code execution can introduce **injection vulnerabilities**.

Best practices include **limiting meta-programming to necessary cases** and **leveraging strong type systems** for safety.

Conclusion

Meta-programming in functional programming provides **powerful tools for code generation, optimization, and abstraction**. Techniques like **macros, type-level programming, lazy evaluation, and DSLs** enable **efficient, declarative, and reusable** code.

From **compiler optimizations to functional DSLs**, meta-programming plays a critical role in reducing **boilerplate, enhancing performance, and ensuring correctness**. While it introduces challenges, **functional programming paradigms ensure safety and composability**, making meta-programming a **cornerstone of modern functional software development**.

Mastering meta-programming opens new possibilities for **high-performance, type-safe, and extensible** functional applications, driving innovation in **compilers, reactive systems, and AI-driven program synthesis**.

Chapter 9: Best Practices and Performance Optimization

Writing Clean and Readable Functional Code

Writing clean and readable functional code is essential for maintainability, collaboration, and long-term project success. Functional programming (FP) emphasizes immutability, declarative patterns, and pure functions, which contribute to more predictable and testable code. However, writing functional code that is both elegant and comprehensible requires adherence to best practices.

1. Favoring Pure Functions

A pure function:

- Always returns the same output for the same input.
- Has no side effects (does not modify global state, mutate parameters, or interact with external dependencies).

Example of a Pure Function in JavaScript:

```
const add = (a, b) => a + b;
console.log(add(2, 3)); // 5
```

Pure functions improve code predictability and testability. They can be composed together without unexpected behaviors.

2. Using Immutability for Safer Data Handling

Immutability prevents data structures from being changed after their creation, reducing unexpected state modifications.

Avoiding Mutation:

```
let numbers = [1, 2, 3];
numbers.push(4); // Mutates the array
```

Using Immutability:

```
const numbers = [1, 2, 3];

const newNumbers = [...numbers, 4]; // Creates a new array

console.log(newNumbers); // [1, 2, 3, 4]
```

In languages like JavaScript, the `spread` operator and methods like `map`, `filter`, and `reduce` help maintain immutability.

3. Leveraging Function Composition

Function composition is a core functional programming technique where smaller functions are combined to form complex operations.

Traditional Approach (Imperative)

```
function toUpperCase(str) {

  return str.toUpperCase();

}


function exclaim(str) {

  return str + "!";

}


function transform(str) {

  return exclaim(toUpperCase(str));

}


console.log(transform("hello")); // "HELLO!"
```

Using Function Composition

With libraries like Ramda or lodash/fp, function composition becomes more elegant:

```
import { compose } from 'ramda';

const transform = compose(
  str => str + "!",
  str => str.toUpperCase()
);

console.log(transform("hello")); // "HELLO!"
```

This approach makes transformations modular and reusable.

4. Avoiding Deeply Nested Functions

Deep nesting reduces readability. Instead, prefer flat structures.

Nested Approach (Difficult to Read)

```
function processArray(arr) {
  return arr.map(x => {
    if (x > 10) {
      return x * 2;
    } else {
      return x + 5;
    }
  }
```

```
    });

}
```

Refactored Using Ternary Operator

```
const processArray = arr => arr.map(x => (x > 10 ? x * 2 : x + 5));
```

Flattening structures leads to better readability.

5. Using Declarative Code Over Imperative Code

Declarative code describes *what* should happen rather than *how* it happens.

Imperative Approach

```
const numbers = [1, 2, 3, 4, 5];

let total = 0;

for (let i = 0; i < numbers.length; i++) {

   total += numbers[i];

}
console.log(total);
```

Declarative Approach

```
const total = numbers.reduce((sum, num) => sum + num, 0);
console.log(total);
```

Declarative programming reduces boilerplate and enhances clarity.

6. Using Higher-Order Functions for Reusability

Higher-order functions take functions as arguments or return functions.

Example: Filtering with a Higher-Order Function

```
const isEven = num => num % 2 === 0;

const filterArray = (arr, predicate) => arr.filter(predicate);


console.log(filterArray([1, 2, 3, 4, 5], isEven)); // [2, 4]
```

Higher-order functions abstract logic, making it reusable.

7. Keeping Functions Small and Focused

Each function should handle one responsibility. Large functions are harder to understand and debug.

Example of a Large Function (Bad Practice)

```
function processUser(user) {

  let fullName = user.firstName + " " + user.lastName;

  let ageInDays = user.age * 365;

  let status = user.age > 18 ? "adult" : "minor";

  return { fullName, ageInDays, status };

}
```

Refactored into Smaller Functions

```
const getFullName = user => `${user.firstName} ${user.lastName}`;

const getAgeInDays = user => user.age * 365;
```

```
const getStatus = user => (user.age > 18 ? "adult" : "minor");


const processUser = user => ({

  fullName: getFullName(user),

  ageInDays: getAgeInDays(user),

  status: getStatus(user),

});
```

This improves modularity and reusability.

8. Handling Errors Functionally

Functional programming avoids exceptions and instead uses monads like `Option` or `Either`.

Example Using JavaScript's Optional Chaining

```
const getUserName = user => user?.name ?? "Guest";

console.log(getUserName({ name: "Alice" })); // "Alice"

console.log(getUserName(null)); // "Guest"
```

This avoids runtime errors from missing properties.

9. Using Functional Libraries

Libraries like `Ramda`, `Lodash/fp`, and `Immutable.js` provide functional utilities that streamline code.

Example Using Ramda for Mapping

```
import { map } from 'ramda';
```

```
const doubleNumbers = map(x => x * 2);

console.log(doubleNumbers([1, 2, 3])); // [2, 4, 6]
```

These libraries simplify functional operations.

10. Writing Tests for Functional Code

Functional code is inherently testable due to its deterministic nature. Use unit tests to verify behavior.

Example: Jest Test for a Pure Function

```
const add = (a, b) => a + b;


test("adds numbers correctly", () => {

  expect(add(2, 3)).toBe(5);

  expect(add(-1, 1)).toBe(0);

});
```

Testing ensures reliability in functional programs.

Conclusion

Writing clean and readable functional code involves using pure functions, immutability, function composition, declarative patterns, and higher-order functions. By adhering to these best practices, developers can create more maintainable, scalable, and testable applications.

Performance Considerations in Functional Programming

Performance is a critical factor in software development, and functional programming (FP) introduces unique considerations due to its emphasis on immutability, recursion, and higher-order functions. While functional programming promotes maintainability and correctness, certain patterns can introduce inefficiencies if not carefully managed. This section explores performance concerns in FP, strategies for optimization, and best practices to ensure efficient execution.

1. Understanding Performance Challenges in Functional Programming

Functional programming presents distinct performance challenges that stem from its core principles:

- **Immutability:** Prevents direct modification of data structures, leading to additional memory usage.
- **Recursion:** Preferred over loops in FP, but deep recursion can cause stack overflows.
- **Lazy Evaluation:** Can defer computation, but may lead to excessive memory consumption if improperly managed.
- **Garbage Collection:** Frequent object creation increases pressure on the garbage collector.

Understanding these challenges is crucial when optimizing functional code.

---

2. Optimizing Immutability-Related Performance Issues

Immutability ensures data consistency but can lead to performance overhead due to the creation of new objects instead of modifying existing ones.

2.1 Avoiding Unnecessary Copying

In JavaScript, naive immutability can lead to excessive copying:

```
const addElement = (arr, element) => [...arr, element];


const numbers = [1, 2, 3];

const newNumbers = addElement(numbers, 4); // Creates a new array
```

For large arrays, copying data every time can be expensive. **Persistent data structures** provide efficient immutability.

2.2 Using Persistent Data Structures

Libraries like **Immutable.js** or **Mori** provide optimized data structures:

```
import { List } from 'immutable';


const list = List([1, 2, 3]);

const newList = list.push(4);


console.log(list.toArray()); // [1, 2, 3]

console.log(newList.toArray()); // [1, 2, 3, 4]
```

Persistent data structures share unchanged parts of the structure, improving performance.

---

3. Optimizing Recursion to Prevent Stack Overflows

Functional programming favors recursion over loops, but deep recursion can cause stack overflows.

3.1 Problem with Regular Recursion

```
function factorial(n) {

  if (n === 0) return 1;

  return n * factorial(n - 1);

}


console.log(factorial(5)); // 120
```

For large n, this can cause a **stack overflow**.

3.2 Using Tail Call Optimization (TCO)

Some languages (like Scala and Haskell) support **tail call optimization**, which prevents stack overflows by reusing stack frames.

In JavaScript (ES6+), TCO works in strict mode with proper tail calls:

```
"use strict";

function factorial(n, acc = 1) {

  if (n === 0) return acc;

  return factorial(n - 1, n * acc);

}

console.log(factorial(10000)); // Works without stack overflow
```

However, since most JavaScript engines lack TCO support, using **iteration** or **trampolines** can help.

---

4. Avoiding Performance Issues with Higher-Order Functions

Higher-order functions like `map`, `filter`, and `reduce` are essential in FP but can lead to performance bottlenecks if chained excessively.

4.1 Inefficient Chaining of Array Methods

```
const numbers = [1, 2, 3, 4, 5];


const result = numbers

  .map(n => n * 2)

  .filter(n => n > 5)

  .reduce((sum, n) => sum + n, 0);
```

Each function creates a new array, leading to unnecessary memory allocations.

4.2 Using Transducers for Efficient Processing

Transducers optimize function chaining by avoiding intermediate collections.

```
import { transduce, map, filter } from "ramda";

const transformer = transduce(

  (acc, val) => acc + val,

  0,

  [map(n => n * 2), filter(n => n > 5)]

);



console.log(transformer(numbers)); // Optimized execution
```

This approach minimizes memory overhead.

---

5. Managing Lazy Evaluation and Avoiding Memory Leaks

Some FP languages like Haskell use **lazy evaluation**, which defers computation until needed. While efficient, it can lead to memory leaks if large structures accumulate.

5.1 Understanding Lazy Evaluation

Consider a **lazy sequence** in Python:

```
def infinite_numbers(start):

    while True:

        yield start

        start += 1
```

```
gen = infinite_numbers(1)

print(next(gen))   # 1

print(next(gen))   # 2
```

This generates numbers **on demand** without storing an entire sequence in memory.

5.2 Avoiding Memory Leaks in Lazy Evaluation

Improperly retaining references to lazy sequences can cause memory bloat.

Bad practice:

```
const lazyArray = Array.from({ length: 1e6 }, (_, i) => i); // Huge
array in memory
```

Better approach using generators:

```
function* numberGenerator() {

  let i = 0;

  while (true) yield i++;

}
```

```
const gen = numberGenerator();

console.log(gen.next().value); // 0

console.log(gen.next().value); // 1
```

This approach efficiently handles infinite sequences without memory overflow.

6. Optimizing Functional Code in Large-Scale Applications

Functional programming can sometimes struggle in large-scale applications due to excessive allocations and garbage collection pressure.

6.1 Memoization for Performance Boost

Memoization stores previously computed results to avoid redundant calculations.

```
const memoize = fn => {

  const cache = {};

  return (...args) => {

    const key = JSON.stringify(args);

    if (cache[key]) return cache[key];

    return (cache[key] = fn(...args));

  };

};
```

```
const fib = memoize(n => (n <= 1 ? n : fib(n - 1) + fib(n - 2)));
```

```
console.log(fib(40)); // Computed efficiently
```

Memoization **significantly speeds up** recursive calculations.

6.2 Using Parallel Processing and Lazy Pipelines

Parallelism can speed up computations in functional programs.

Example using `parallel` in JavaScript (Node.js Worker Threads):

```
const { Worker, isMainThread, parentPort } =
require('worker_threads');
```

```
if (isMainThread) {

  const worker = new Worker(__filename);

  worker.on('message', msg => console.log("Result:", msg));

  worker.postMessage(100);

} else {

  parentPort.on('message', num => parentPort.postMessage(num * 2));

}
```

This utilizes worker threads for parallel execution.

---

7. Hybrid Approaches: Combining Functional and Imperative Techniques

While FP provides elegant abstractions, a **hybrid approach** often balances performance and clarity.

7.1 Using Mutable Data Where Necessary

Immutable structures sometimes introduce overhead. For performance-sensitive sections, limited mutability can help.

```
let arr = [];

for (let i = 0; i < 1000000; i++) {

  arr.push(i);

}
```

This is more efficient than recursively constructing a new array.

7.2 Choosing the Right Tool for the Job

- Use FP for modularity, safety, and testability.
- Use imperative constructs where raw performance is critical.

Conclusion

Performance considerations in functional programming require balancing immutability, recursion, lazy evaluation, and higher-order functions. While FP enhances maintainability and correctness, improper usage can degrade performance. By adopting persistent data structures, optimizing recursion, leveraging transducers, using memoization, and selectively employing imperative techniques, developers can ensure efficient functional programs.

Debugging and Testing Functional Code

Debugging and testing are critical aspects of software development, ensuring that functional programs are correct, reliable, and maintainable. Functional programming (FP) introduces unique challenges and advantages when it comes to debugging and testing due to immutability, pure functions, and the absence of side effects. In this section, we explore best practices, tools, and techniques for debugging and testing functional code efficiently.

---

1. Debugging Functional Code: Challenges and Solutions

Debugging in functional programming can be different from traditional debugging due to the reliance on expressions rather than statements, immutability, and function composition. Here are some common debugging challenges and strategies to overcome them.

1.1 Difficulty of Debugging Composed Functions

Functional programs rely heavily on **function composition**, making it difficult to track the flow of data when issues arise.

Example of complex function composition:

```
const processData = compose(

  filter(x => x % 2 === 0),

  map(x => x * 2),

  reduce((acc, x) => acc + x, 0)

);


console.log(processData([1, 2, 3, 4, 5])); // ???
```

Solution: Use **logging functions** within compositions.

```
const log = label => x => (console.log(`${label}:`, x), x);


const processData = compose(

  log("After Filter"),

  filter(x => x % 2 === 0),

  log("After Map"),

  map(x => x * 2),

  log("After Reduce"),

  reduce((acc, x) => acc + x, 0)
);


console.log(processData([1, 2, 3, 4, 5]));
```

By inserting `log` functions, we can observe transformations at each step.

1.2 Debugging Higher-Order Functions

Higher-order functions can obscure where errors occur.

Example:

```
const applyFunction = (fn, arr) => arr.map(fn);

const square = x => x * x;

console.log(applyFunction(square, [1, "a", 3])); // NaN error
```

The error is due to `"a"`, but finding the issue can be tricky.

Solution: Use **type checks** and debugging functions.

```
const safeSquare = x => (typeof x === "number" ? x * x :
console.warn("Invalid input:", x));
```

```
console.log(applyFunction(safeSquare, [1, "a", 3]));
```

This approach helps identify incorrect values early.

1.3 Debugging Lazy Evaluations

Some functional languages, like Haskell, use **lazy evaluation**, delaying execution until necessary. This can make debugging difficult.

Example of lazy evaluation in Python:

```
def numbers():
    i = 0
    while True:
        yield i
        i += 1

gen = numbers()
print(next(gen)) # 0
print(next(gen)) # 1
```

Lazy generators do not execute immediately, so **tracing** their behavior can be difficult.

Solution: Force evaluation using debugging functions.

```
print(list(islice(numbers(), 10))) # Prints first 10 elements
```

In JavaScript, use `.take()` or explicit iteration:

```
const take = (n, iter) => [...iter].slice(0, n);
console.log(take(5, numberGenerator())); // Debugging output
```

---

2. Logging Strategies in Functional Code

Logging is essential for debugging. However, FP discourages side effects, making traditional logging challenging.

2.1 Using Logging Without Side Effects

Avoid:

```
const add = (a, b) => {

  console.log(`Adding ${a} and ${b}`);

  return a + b;

};
```

This violates **purity** since `console.log` is a side effect.

Functional Approach:

```
const log = fn => (...args) => {

  const result = fn(...args);
```

```
console.log(`Function ${fn.name} called with ${args}, returned
${result}`);

    return result;

};


const add = (a, b) => a + b;

const loggedAdd = log(add);


console.log(loggedAdd(2, 3)); // Debugging without breaking purity
```

---

3. Functional Testing Strategies

Testing in FP is often easier due to **pure functions**, predictable outputs, and reduced reliance on state.

3.1 Unit Testing Pure Functions

Pure functions are ideal for unit testing because they always return the same output for a given input.

Example: Jest test for a pure function

```
const add = (a, b) => a + b;


test("adds numbers correctly", () => {

    expect(add(2, 3)).toBe(5);

    expect(add(-1, 1)).toBe(0);

});
```

Since pure functions have no dependencies, tests are **fast and reliable**.

3.2 Property-Based Testing

Instead of writing individual test cases, **property-based testing** generates test inputs dynamically.

Using `fast-check` in JavaScript:

```
import fc from "fast-check";
```

```
const add = (a, b) => a + b;
```

```
test("addition is commutative", () => {
  fc.assert(fc.property(fc.integer(), fc.integer(), (a, b) => {
    return add(a, b) === add(b, a);
  }));
});
```

This ensures the function holds for a **wide range of inputs**.

3.3 Testing Higher-Order Functions

Higher-order functions should be tested with **mock functions**.

Example:

```
test("applyFunction applies the given function", () => {
  const mockFn = jest.fn(x => x * 2);
  const result = applyFunction(mockFn, [1, 2, 3]);
```

```
expect(mockFn).toHaveBeenCalledTimes(3);

expect(result).toEqual([2, 4, 6]);

});
```

Mock functions allow verifying if a function was called the correct number of times and with expected arguments.

---

4. Debugging and Testing Asynchronous Functional Code

Functional programs often use **promises** and **async/await** for asynchronous tasks. Debugging async functions requires special care.

4.1 Debugging Async Functions with Logging

```
const fetchData = async url => {

  console.log(`Fetching from ${url}`);

  const response = await fetch(url);

  return response.json();

};



fetchData("https://api.example.com");
```

Adding logs inside async functions helps track execution.

4.2 Testing Async Functions

Using Jest:

```
const fetchData = async () => "Hello, World!";
```

```
test("fetchData returns correct data", async () => {

  await expect(fetchData()).resolves.toBe("Hello, World!");

});
```

Async testing ensures correct handling of **promises and errors**.

5. Functional Debugging Tools

Several tools assist in debugging functional applications.

5.1 Browser DevTools for Functional Debugging

- Chrome DevTools allows **breakpoints in higher-order functions**.
- `console.trace()` shows the function call stack.

5.2 Debugging Functional Code in Node.js

Use `node --inspect` for debugging Node.js applications.

5.3 Functional Debugging Libraries

- **Ramda Debugging Helpers** provide better insights into function calls.
- **Redux DevTools** for state debugging in React functional applications.

Conclusion

Debugging and testing functional code require a different mindset compared to imperative programming. By leveraging pure functions, structured logging, property-based testing, and specialized debugging tools, developers can efficiently maintain functional programs. Following best practices ensures clean, bug-free, and maintainable functional applications.

Optimizing Functional Code for Large-Scale Applications

Functional programming (FP) provides a powerful approach to software development by promoting immutability, pure functions, and declarative patterns. However, scaling functional code efficiently requires optimizations in execution speed, memory usage, and concurrency. Large-scale applications often face performance bottlenecks due to excessive function calls, inefficient data structures, and uncontrolled recursion. This section explores techniques to optimize functional code, ensuring efficiency while maintaining the benefits of FP.

1. Managing Performance in Pure Functions

Pure functions improve code reliability, but excessive function calls can lead to inefficiencies. The following strategies help maintain performance while adhering to FP principles.

1.1 Memoization for Reducing Redundant Computation

Memoization caches function results to avoid repeated calculations.

Example: Naive Recursive Fibonacci (Inefficient)

```
const fib = n => (n <= 1 ? n : fib(n - 1) + fib(n - 2));
```

```
console.log(fib(40)); // Extremely slow due to redundant calculations
```

Optimized with Memoization

```
const memoize = fn => {
  const cache = {};
  return (...args) => {
    const key = JSON.stringify(args);
    if (cache[key]) return cache[key];
    return (cache[key] = fn(...args));
  };
};
```

```
const fib = memoize(n => (n <= 1 ? n : fib(n - 1) + fib(n - 2)));
```

```
console.log(fib(40)); // Runs significantly faster
```

Memoization dramatically reduces redundant computations, making recursive functions practical.

1.2 Optimizing Function Composition

Function composition enhances modularity but may create unnecessary intermediate data structures.

Inefficient Composition (Creates Intermediate Arrays)

```
const processNumbers = numbers =>

  numbers

    .map(n => n * 2)

    .filter(n => n > 10)

    .reduce((sum, n) => sum + n, 0);


console.log(processNumbers([1, 5, 10, 15]));
```

Each method (map, filter, reduce) creates a new array, increasing memory usage.

Optimized with Transducers

```
import { compose, map, filter, transduce } from "ramda";


const processNumbers = transduce(

  compose(
```

```
  map(n => n * 2),

  filter(n => n > 10)

),

(sum, n) => sum + n,

0

);


console.log(processNumbers([1, 5, 10, 15]));
```

Transducers eliminate intermediate arrays, improving performance.

---

2. Handling Large Data Efficiently

Processing large data structures efficiently is critical in FP. Techniques like **lazy evaluation**, **persistent data structures**, and **parallel processing** help optimize memory usage.

2.1 Lazy Evaluation for Efficient Computation

Eager evaluation computes all values immediately, consuming unnecessary memory.

Example: Eager Computation (Wasteful)

```
const range = n => [...Array(n).keys()];

const doubled = range(1e6).map(x => x * 2); // Creates a massive array
in memory
```

Lazy Evaluation Using Generators

```
function* range(n) {

  for (let i = 0; i < n; i++) yield i;
```

```
}


function* double(iter) {

  for (let n of iter) yield n * 2;

}


const numbers = double(range(1e6));

console.log([...numbers].slice(0,  10));  //  Lazily  processes  only
needed elements
```

Lazy evaluation defers computation until necessary, reducing memory overhead.

2.2 Using Persistent Data Structures

Immutability in FP can lead to inefficient memory usage if data is copied frequently. **Persistent data structures** optimize immutable operations by sharing unchanged portions.

Example: Traditional Immutable Data Structure (Inefficient)

```
const arr = [1, 2, 3];

const newArr = [...arr, 4]; // Creates a full copy in memory
```

Optimized with Persistent Data Structures (Immutable.js)

```
import { List } from "immutable";


const list = List([1, 2, 3]);

const newList = list.push(4); // Efficiently shares memory
```

```
console.log(newList.toArray()); // [1, 2, 3, 4]
```

Persistent data structures ensure immutability without excessive memory consumption.

---

3. Optimizing Recursion to Prevent Stack Overflows

Recursion is a fundamental FP technique, but deep recursion can cause stack overflow errors.

3.1 Using Tail Call Optimization (TCO)

Some languages optimize recursive calls through **Tail Call Optimization (TCO)**, which reuses the stack frame instead of adding new ones.

Non-TCO Recursion (Can Cause Stack Overflow)

```
function factorial(n) {

  if (n === 0) return 1;

  return n * factorial(n - 1);

}

console.log(factorial(10000)); // Stack overflow
```

Optimized with Tail Recursion

```
"use strict";


function factorial(n, acc = 1) {

  if (n === 0) return acc;

  return factorial(n - 1, n * acc);

}
```

```
console.log(factorial(10000)); // Optimized, no stack overflow
```

---

4. Parallel and Asynchronous Functional Execution

Functional programs can benefit from parallel execution and concurrency optimizations.

4.1 Parallel Processing for Large Datasets

Map-reduce paradigms allow efficient parallel execution.

Example: Parallel Execution in JavaScript (Node.js Worker Threads)

```
const { Worker, isMainThread, parentPort } = require("worker_threads");

if (isMainThread) {
  const worker = new Worker(__filename);
  worker.on("message", msg => console.log("Result:", msg));
  worker.postMessage(100);
} else {
  parentPort.on("message", num => parentPort.postMessage(num * 2));
}
```

Worker threads distribute computation across CPU cores, improving efficiency.

4.2 Using Async Functional Patterns

Asynchronous functional programming helps optimize non-blocking operations.

Example: Asynchronous Composition Using Promises

```
const fetchData = async url => {

  const response = await fetch(url);

  return response.json();

};


const processResponse = compose(

  data => console.log("Processed:", data),

  fetchData

);


processResponse("https://api.example.com");
```

Asynchronous function composition enables efficient I/O operations.

---

5. Optimizing Functional Code for Real-World Applications

To ensure functional code scales efficiently in production, consider the following:

5.1 Avoiding Overuse of Higher-Order Functions

- Excessive `.map().filter().reduce()` calls can slow down performance.
- Use **transducers** for batch processing.

5.2 Profiling and Benchmarking Functional Code

- Use **Node.js Performance Hooks** or `console.time()`.

```
console.time("Execution Time");

someExpensiveFunction();

console.timeEnd("Execution Time");
```

- Profile execution with `Chrome DevTools` or `Flamegraphs`.

5.3 Combining Functional and Imperative Techniques

- FP is ideal for business logic and transformations.
- **Use imperative loops** when raw performance is needed.

```
let sum = 0;

for (let i = 0; i < arr.length; i++) {

  sum += arr[i]; // More efficient than reduce for large arrays

}
```

Conclusion

Optimizing functional code for large-scale applications requires balancing immutability, recursion, concurrency, and efficient data structures. Using **memoization, persistent data structures, tail recursion, lazy evaluation, transducers, and parallel processing**, developers can enhance performance while retaining the benefits of functional programming. These optimizations ensure scalability, maintainability, and efficiency in complex systems.

Hybrid Approaches: Combining Functional and Object-Oriented Programming

Functional programming (FP) and object-oriented programming (OOP) are often viewed as opposing paradigms, but they can be combined effectively to leverage the strengths of both. In real-world applications, pure functional code can sometimes lead to performance issues or complexity in state management, while OOP alone can result in code that is difficult to test and maintain. By adopting a hybrid approach, developers can benefit from **immutability, pure functions, and composition** while also leveraging **encapsulation, polymorphism, and object management** where appropriate.

1. Understanding the Differences and Overlaps Between FP and OOP

Before exploring how FP and OOP can complement each other, it's important to understand their key characteristics.

1.1 Core Features of Functional Programming

- **Pure functions**: Functions with no side effects and deterministic outputs.
- **Immutability**: Data structures cannot be modified once created.
- **Function composition**: Smaller functions are combined to form complex operations.
- **First-class functions**: Functions are treated as values and can be passed around.

1.2 Core Features of Object-Oriented Programming

- **Encapsulation**: Grouping related data and methods in objects.
- **Inheritance**: Sharing behavior across different objects via parent-child relationships.
- **Polymorphism**: Defining methods that work across multiple object types.
- **Stateful objects**: Objects maintain and modify their own state.

1.3 Where FP and OOP Overlap

Despite their differences, FP and OOP share some principles:

- **Encapsulation vs. Closures**: Both manage state and hide implementation details.
- **Composition vs. Inheritance**: FP favors composition, while OOP traditionally favors inheritance.
- **Modular Design**: Both paradigms emphasize modular, reusable code.

By combining these paradigms, we can create **scalable, maintainable, and efficient** software systems.

---

2. Functional Objects: Using Objects with Functional Principles

One of the simplest ways to combine FP and OOP is to write **functional objects**, where objects are immutable and their methods follow functional principles.

2.1 Using Immutable Objects in OOP

In OOP, objects typically have mutable state:

```
class Person {

  constructor(name, age) {

    this.name = name;

    this.age = age;

  }
```

```
  celebrateBirthday() {

    this.age++; // Mutates state

  }

}
```

Refactored using immutability (Functional Object):

```
class Person {

  constructor(name, age) {

    this.name = name;

    this.age = age;

  }


  celebrateBirthday() {

    return new Person(this.name, this.age + 1); // Returns a new
object

  }

}
```

```
const john = new Person("John", 30);

const olderJohn = john.celebrateBirthday();

console.log(john.age); // 30 (original object remains unchanged)

console.log(olderJohn.age); // 31 (new object created)
```

This approach maintains **immutability** while using an OOP structure.

---

3. Using Functional Composition Within OOP

Instead of relying on inheritance, FP prefers **composition**, which allows objects to be built from smaller, reusable functions.

3.1 Avoiding Inheritance with Composition

Traditional OOP Inheritance (Less Flexible)

```
class Animal {

  speak() {

    console.log("Some generic sound");

  }

}


class Dog extends Animal {

  speak() {

    console.log("Bark");

  }

}
```

Refactored using Function Composition

```
const makeSpeak = sound => () => console.log(sound);


const dog = {

  speak: makeSpeak("Bark")
```

```
};
```

```
dog.speak(); // "Bark"
```

By composing behavior from functions instead of using inheritance, the code is **more flexible and reusable**.

---

4. Combining Higher-Order Functions with Object Methods

Higher-order functions (HOFs) are a key feature of FP and can be used in OOP to create reusable logic.

4.1 Using HOFs to Modify Object Behavior

```
const withLogging = fn => (...args) => {

  console.log(`Called with arguments: ${args}`);

  return fn(...args);

};
```

```
class Calculator {

  add(a, b) {

    return a + b;

  }

}
```

```
const calc = new Calculator();

calc.add = withLogging(calc.add);
```

```
console.log(calc.add(2, 3)); // Logs input and output
```

This **decorator pattern** allows us to wrap object methods with additional behavior, following **functional principles**.

---

5. Managing State in a Hybrid Approach

State management is a common challenge in large applications. FP prefers **immutable state** and **pure functions**, while OOP often relies on **mutable objects**.

5.1 Using Pure Functions for State Management

Instead of modifying state directly:

```
class Counter {

  constructor(count) {

    this.count = count;

  }


  increment() {

    this.count++; // Mutates state

  }

}
```

Use a functional approach:

```
const increment = state => ({ ...state, count: state.count + 1 });


const state = { count: 0 };
```

```
const newState = increment(state);
```

```
console.log(state.count); // 0
```

```
console.log(newState.count); // 1
```

This ensures **predictable state transitions**.

5.2 Hybrid State Management: Using Redux in OOP-Based Applications

Redux, a functional state management tool, can be integrated into OOP applications.

Redux Reducer (Functional Approach)

```
const counterReducer = (state = { count: 0 }, action) => {

  switch (action.type) {

    case "INCREMENT":

      return { ...state, count: state.count + 1 };

    default:

      return state;

  }

};
```

Even in object-based applications, Redux provides a **functional state management** layer.

---

6. Parallel and Asynchronous Functional Object Handling

OOP is often used for managing complex object graphs, while FP excels at **asynchronous and parallel processing**.

6.1 Handling Asynchronous Operations in a Hybrid Approach

Instead of using callbacks in objects:

```
class API {

  fetchData(url, callback) {

    fetch(url).then(response => response.json()).then(callback);

  }

}
```

Use a **functional approach with Promises**:

```
class API {

  fetchData(url) {

    return fetch(url).then(response => response.json());

  }

}
```

```
const api = new API();

api.fetchData("https://api.example.com").then(console.log);
```

This removes **side effects** and makes the API more **composable**.

---

7. Choosing the Right Approach for Scalability

Each approach has trade-offs:

Feature	Functional Programming	Object-Oriented Programming

State Management	Immutable data, pure functions	Mutable objects, encapsulation
Code Reusability	Function composition, HOFs	Inheritance, polymorphism
Concurrency	Stateless, easy to parallelize	Often stateful, requires careful management
Debugging	Predictable, fewer side effects	More complexity due to state mutations

By combining FP and OOP, we can **choose the best tool for each scenario**.

Conclusion

Hybrid approaches leverage the best of both worlds: the **modularity and predictability of FP** with the **encapsulation and structure of OOP**. By using **immutable objects, function composition, higher-order functions, and functional state management**, developers can create maintainable and scalable software. This balance ensures applications remain **flexible, efficient, and easy to reason about** in real-world use cases.

Chapter 10: Future of Functional Programming

Trends and Innovations in Functional Programming

Functional programming (FP) has continued to evolve, shaping the way software is written and influencing various domains, from web development to artificial intelligence (AI). As computing paradigms shift towards concurrency, distributed systems, and data-intensive applications, functional programming provides robust solutions to modern challenges. This section explores the latest trends and innovations in functional programming and how they are shaping the future of software development.

The Rise of Functional Programming in Mainstream Development

Historically, functional programming was considered an academic pursuit, mainly used in niche applications. However, over the past decade, mainstream programming languages have incorporated functional features, demonstrating FP's growing importance.

- **JavaScript (ES6+):** Introduction of arrow functions, higher-order functions like `map`, `reduce`, and `filter`, and immutability-focused libraries like Immutable.js.
- **Python:** Adoption of functional constructs such as list comprehensions, lambda functions, and functools for higher-order operations.
- **Java and C#:** Features like lambda expressions, streams, and functional interfaces have significantly improved the expressiveness of these traditionally object-oriented languages.
- **Kotlin and Swift:** These languages offer robust support for immutability, first-class functions, and functional combinators, making them more functional-friendly.
- **Rust:** Borrowing from FP principles, Rust emphasizes immutability and pure functions for safer, concurrent programming.
- **Scala, Haskell, and Clojure:** These languages remain at the forefront of functional programming, serving as inspiration for modern language features.

With FP principles appearing in general-purpose programming, developers are increasingly adopting immutable data structures, referential transparency, and declarative programming in everyday software development.

Functional Programming in Concurrency and Parallelism

Modern applications demand highly concurrent and parallel processing capabilities. Functional programming, with its emphasis on immutability and pure functions, is particularly suited for such workloads.

- **Immutable State:** Since functional programs avoid mutable state, race conditions and side effects are minimized, making it easier to reason about concurrency.

- **Actor Model:** Languages like Erlang and frameworks like Akka in Scala leverage the actor model for fault-tolerant distributed computing.
- **Software Transactional Memory (STM):** Used in Haskell, STM enables safe and efficient memory transactions without traditional locks.
- **Reactive Programming:** The rise of Functional Reactive Programming (FRP) enables developers to build highly responsive applications that react to real-time data streams.

Functional programming is also a natural fit for **multi-core processing** since pure functions can be easily parallelized without concern for data corruption or synchronization issues.

Serverless Computing and Functional Programming

Serverless computing, which abstracts infrastructure management from developers, is another area where functional programming is gaining traction.

- **Stateless Execution:** Serverless platforms like AWS Lambda and Google Cloud Functions work best with stateless functions, aligning perfectly with functional programming paradigms.
- **Event-Driven Architecture:** FP's ability to handle event streams and data pipelines makes it ideal for reactive serverless applications.
- **Scalability and Cost Efficiency:** Pure functions can be independently executed, allowing serverless functions to scale horizontally without interference.

As cloud providers continue to optimize serverless environments, functional programming will play an increasingly vital role in building efficient, cost-effective, and scalable applications.

Functional Programming in Data Science and Machine Learning

Data science, artificial intelligence, and machine learning (ML) rely on handling large volumes of data efficiently. Functional programming principles, such as immutability and function composition, simplify data transformations and ensure reproducibility.

- **Data Pipelines:** Functional constructs like `map`, `reduce`, and `filter` are extensively used in data processing frameworks like Apache Spark and Pandas.
- **Laziness and Efficiency:** Lazy evaluation allows processing massive datasets efficiently, loading only what is needed.
- **Deterministic Computations:** FP ensures consistent results, which is crucial for scientific computing and ML model training.
- **Declarative ML Pipelines:** Libraries like TensorFlow and PyTorch use functional paradigms to construct computation graphs for deep learning.

As AI continues to evolve, functional programming will provide the necessary tools for building robust, scalable, and efficient data processing applications.

Domain-Specific Languages (DSLs) and Functional Programming

Functional programming is widely used for designing Domain-Specific Languages (DSLs), which are specialized languages tailored for particular domains.

- **Haskell and Scala:** These languages are frequently used to build powerful DSLs due to their strong type systems and functional constructs.
- **Graph Query Languages:** Query languages like GraphQL and Datalog borrow FP concepts to enable expressive data querying.
- **Infrastructure as Code (IaC):** Tools like Terraform and Nix use FP principles to define infrastructure declaratively.

The use of FP in DSLs continues to grow as industries demand more specialized, expressive, and maintainable programming languages.

Category Theory and Advanced Functional Programming

Category theory, a mathematical foundation for functional programming, has influenced modern software development by providing structured abstractions.

- **Functors, Monads, and Applicatives:** These constructs enable safe and composable effect handling, preventing runtime errors and ensuring predictable computations.
- **Higher-Kinded Types:** Found in languages like Haskell and Scala, higher-kinded types improve code reuse and type safety.
- **Type-Level Programming:** Advancements in dependent types, seen in Idris and Scala 3, allow for more expressive compile-time checks.

The increasing adoption of category-theoretic concepts will drive the future of functional programming, leading to more expressive and mathematically sound software design.

The Integration of Functional Programming with Blockchain and Cryptography

Blockchain and cryptographic applications benefit from the deterministic nature of functional programming.

- **Smart Contracts:** Languages like Plutus (Haskell-based) and Michelson (used in Tezos) leverage FP's mathematical precision to build verifiable smart contracts.
- **Formal Verification:** FP's strong type systems and immutable state ensure that cryptographic algorithms and blockchain protocols are more secure.
- **Decentralized Computation:** Functional principles align well with distributed ledger technology, providing a foundation for secure, parallel computations.

With the rapid growth of blockchain technology, functional programming is becoming a key player in secure, decentralized systems.

The Role of Functional Programming in AI and Quantum Computing

Emerging fields like artificial intelligence and quantum computing are beginning to incorporate functional programming principles.

- **Quantum Functional Languages:** Languages like Q# (Microsoft) and Silq use FP concepts to manage quantum state and superposition.

- **AI Model Explainability:** Functional programming ensures that AI models remain composable, interpretable, and modular.
- **Parallel AI Computation:** Functional programming enhances parallel execution in AI models, optimizing performance for large-scale deep learning.

As quantum computing and AI continue to advance, functional programming will provide the necessary abstractions for tackling complex computational challenges.

Conclusion

Functional programming is no longer an obscure, academic paradigm; it is shaping the future of software development across multiple industries. From AI and blockchain to data science and cloud computing, functional principles are enabling developers to write safer, more scalable, and more maintainable code. As programming languages continue to integrate FP concepts, the influence of functional programming will only grow, making it an essential skill for modern software engineers.

By staying informed about these trends and continuously learning about FP advancements, developers can prepare for the future of programming and build more robust, efficient, and scalable systems.

The Rise of Functional Programming in Industry

Functional programming (FP) has transitioned from academic discussions to widespread industry adoption. Companies across various sectors, from finance to gaming, are leveraging functional paradigms to build scalable, maintainable, and efficient software solutions. The shift toward FP is driven by its ability to simplify complex problems, enhance code reliability, and support modern computing demands like concurrency and distributed systems.

This section explores how different industries are adopting functional programming, the benefits they are realizing, and the challenges they face. It also examines case studies of real-world companies that have successfully integrated FP into their development workflow.

Why Industries Are Adopting Functional Programming

The adoption of functional programming in industry is driven by several key advantages:

1. **Immutability and Predictability**
   FP emphasizes immutable data structures, reducing side effects and making it easier to reason about code. This predictability is especially beneficial in environments where data consistency is critical, such as finance and healthcare.
2. **Concurrency and Parallelism**
   With the rise of multi-core processors, FP's inherent support for concurrency makes it an ideal choice for scalable applications. Pure functions ensure thread safety, allowing for efficient parallel execution.
3. **Ease of Testing and Debugging**
   Functional code is often more testable because functions have no hidden

dependencies. This makes unit testing more straightforward and reduces debugging complexity.

4. **Declarative** **and** **Composable** **Code**
FP promotes declarative programming, leading to more readable and maintainable codebases. The ability to compose functions enables modular development and reuse.

5. **Scalability** **and** **Cloud** **Computing**
Functional paradigms align well with serverless computing and microservices architectures, making FP a natural fit for cloud-based applications.

Functional Programming in Various Industries

Finance and FinTech

The finance industry has been one of the earliest adopters of functional programming. Due to its need for high precision, low-latency transactions, and concurrent data processing, financial institutions have embraced FP concepts.

- **Risk Analysis and Quantitative Finance**: Functional languages like Haskell and OCaml are widely used for mathematical modeling and risk assessment.
- **Trading Systems**: Firms like Jane Street use OCaml to develop high-frequency trading systems that require real-time computations with minimal latency.
- **Fraud Detection**: Functional programming simplifies the implementation of machine learning models for fraud detection.

Example of a functional approach to risk assessment using Haskell:

```
type RiskScore = Double


assessRisk :: [Double] -> RiskScore

assessRisk factors = sum (map (* 1.2) factors) / fromIntegral (length
factors)
```

By using pure functions, this risk assessment function ensures determinism and testability.

Web Development and E-Commerce

Modern web applications require scalability and maintainability, and functional programming helps achieve both.

- **Frontend Development**: React, a JavaScript library for building user interfaces, is heavily influenced by functional programming concepts. It uses immutable state management and pure functions.

- **Backend Development**: Functional frameworks like Elixir (built on Erlang) provide highly scalable backend solutions for handling concurrent users.
- **E-Commerce Platforms**: Functional programming helps implement recommendation engines, cart management, and real-time inventory tracking.

An example of a pure function in React:

```
const addToCart = (cart, item) => [...cart, item];

const updatedCart = addToCart(["Laptop", "Mouse"], "Keyboard");

console.log(updatedCart); // ["Laptop", "Mouse", "Keyboard"]
```

The function `addToCart` ensures immutability by creating a new array instead of modifying the original one.

Machine Learning and Artificial Intelligence

Functional programming is increasingly being used in AI and machine learning applications.

- **Data Transformation Pipelines**: FP concepts like function composition and lazy evaluation are beneficial in data preprocessing.
- **Neural Network Design**: Libraries like TensorFlow and PyTorch use declarative programming to define computation graphs.
- **Parallelized Training**: FP's immutability simplifies the parallel training of machine learning models.

Example of function composition in data processing using Python:

```
def normalize(data):

    return [x / max(data) for x in data]


def remove_outliers(data, threshold):

    return [x for x in data if x < threshold]
```

```python
def process_data(data, threshold):

    return normalize(remove_outliers(data, threshold))


data = [10, 50, 200, 30, 500, 20]

cleaned_data = process_data(data, 100)

print(cleaned_data)  # Normalized data after removing outliers
```

Game Development

Functional programming is also finding its place in game development.

- **Game Logic Implementation**: FP simplifies game logic by ensuring deterministic behavior through pure functions.
- **Concurrency for Multiplayer Games**: FP's concurrency capabilities help in handling multiple players and events in real-time.
- **Procedural Generation**: FP's recursive functions and lazy evaluation make procedural content generation efficient.

Example of functional procedural terrain generation using Scala:

```scala
def generateTerrain(seed: Int, size: Int): List[Int] = {

  val random = new scala.util.Random(seed)

  List.fill(size)(random.nextInt(100))

}


val terrain = generateTerrain(42, 10)

println(terrain) // A list of terrain heights
```

By using pure functions, the terrain generation remains deterministic and reproducible.

Healthcare and Bioinformatics

The healthcare sector relies on functional programming for:

- **Medical Imaging Processing**: FP ensures that image transformations are reproducible.
- **Genomic Data Analysis**: Haskell and Scala are used in bioinformatics for analyzing DNA sequences.
- **Predictive Analytics**: FP simplifies the implementation of predictive models for disease detection.

Example of using functional programming for patient data analysis in Scala:

```scala
case class Patient(name: String, age: Int, condition: String)


val patients = List(

  Patient("Alice", 30, "Diabetes"),

  Patient("Bob", 45, "Hypertension"),

  Patient("Charlie", 50, "Healthy")

)


val filteredPatients = patients.filter(_.condition != "Healthy")

println(filteredPatients)
```

This approach ensures immutability and simplifies data transformations.

Challenges in Industry Adoption of Functional Programming

Despite its advantages, FP adoption faces several challenges:

1. **Learning Curve**: Many developers are accustomed to imperative and object-oriented paradigms, making the transition to FP difficult.
2. **Performance Overheads**: While FP provides benefits like immutability and purity, it can introduce performance costs due to frequent memory allocations.
3. **Limited Tooling and Libraries**: Compared to OOP languages, some FP languages have fewer libraries and frameworks.
4. **Legacy System Integration**: Many enterprises rely on OOP-based legacy systems, making full FP adoption challenging.
5. **Recruitment Challenges**: Finding skilled FP developers can be difficult since FP is still less common than imperative programming.

Conclusion

The rise of functional programming in industry is driven by its ability to produce more reliable, scalable, and maintainable software. From finance to healthcare, AI to game development, FP is enabling companies to build high-performance applications while reducing complexity.

Despite some challenges, the increasing adoption of FP in mainstream languages like JavaScript, Python, and Kotlin suggests that its influence will only grow. As businesses continue to prioritize scalability, security, and concurrent computing, functional programming will play a key role in shaping the future of software development.

For developers and organizations looking to stay ahead in the rapidly evolving tech landscape, understanding and integrating functional programming principles will be a valuable investment.

How to Stay Updated with Functional Programming Advancements

Functional programming (FP) is continuously evolving, with new techniques, libraries, and frameworks emerging regularly. Staying updated with the latest advancements is essential for developers who want to deepen their expertise and apply modern FP principles effectively in their projects. This section explores various strategies, resources, and communities that can help developers keep pace with the latest trends in functional programming.

Understanding the Evolution of Functional Programming

Functional programming has come a long way from its early academic roots to widespread industry adoption. To stay updated, developers must understand how FP has evolved and where it is heading.

1. **Mainstream Adoption of FP Concepts**
   Many imperative and object-oriented languages have integrated functional features. JavaScript (ES6+), Python, Java, and C# now support higher-order functions, lambda expressions, and immutable data structures.
2. **Rise of Functional-First Languages**
   Languages such as Haskell, Scala, F#, and Elixir continue to push FP forward by introducing more advanced type systems, category-theory-based abstractions, and better concurrency models.
3. **Performance Optimizations in FP**
   Traditionally, FP was considered less performant due to immutable data structures and recursion overheads. However, advancements in Just-In-Time (JIT) compilation, tail call optimization (TCO), and persistent data structures have significantly improved performance.
4. **Functional Programming in AI and Machine Learning**
   Libraries such as TensorFlow and PyTorch use FP principles to construct declarative computation graphs. The influence of FP in data science is growing rapidly.

By tracking these trends, developers can anticipate changes and incorporate the latest functional programming techniques into their work.

Following Industry-Leading Blogs and Publications

Reading high-quality blogs and publications is one of the best ways to stay informed about the latest advancements in functional programming. Here are some notable sources:

- **Functional Programming Blogs**
    - *Lambda the Ultimate*: Discusses theoretical and practical FP concepts.
    - *The Haskell Blog*: Covers updates and best practices in Haskell.
    - *The Elixir Blog*: Offers insights into Elixir and functional programming in web applications.
    - *Chris Ford's Blog*: Focuses on functional programming in music and other creative applications.
- **Tech Publications**
    - *Medium - Functional Programming Section*: Hosts articles from developers across various FP languages.
    - *Hackernoon - Functional Programming*: Features real-world case studies of FP applications.
    - *InfoQ - Functional Programming*: Covers news on FP languages, tools, and methodologies.

Subscribing to these blogs ensures a steady flow of up-to-date FP knowledge.

Engaging with Functional Programming Communities

Participating in FP communities allows developers to learn from peers, ask questions, and contribute to discussions. Some of the most active FP communities include:

- **Online Forums and Discussion Boards**
    - *Reddit* - r/functionalprogramming
    - *Stack Overflow* - Functional programming tag
    - *Haskell Discourse* - Discussions about Haskell and FP in general
- **Chat Groups and Social Media**
    - *Twitter* - Many FP experts share insights and articles on Twitter.
    - *Discord* - Functional programming communities host real-time discussions.
    - *Slack* - Many FP-related workspaces exist, such as the Elixir and Scala Slack channels.

Engaging in discussions, asking questions, and contributing answers help deepen one's understanding of FP.

Enrolling in Online Courses and Workshops

Learning through structured courses and workshops is an effective way to gain hands-on experience with functional programming. Some of the best platforms offering FP courses include:

- **Udemy and Coursera**
  - *Functional Programming in Scala (Coursera)*
  - *Haskell Fundamentals (Udemy)*
  - *Functional Programming in JavaScript (Udemy)*
- **Pluralsight and Educative**
  - *Elixir for Beginners (Pluralsight)*
  - *Advanced FP Concepts (Educative)*
- **University MOOCs**
  - *MIT's Introduction to Functional Programming*
  - *Stanford's Functional Programming Principles*

Completing these courses builds a strong foundation and keeps developers up-to-date with modern FP practices.

Attending Functional Programming Conferences

Conferences bring together FP experts, researchers, and industry leaders to discuss new advancements and real-world applications. Some of the most popular FP conferences include:

- **Lambda Days**: Covers FP in industry and academia.
- **Haskell eXchange**: Focuses on developments in the Haskell ecosystem.
- **Scala Days**: Dedicated to advancements in Scala and FP techniques.
- **Clojure/conj**: Highlights best practices in Clojure programming.
- **ElixirConf**: Explores Elixir's growth and adoption in production systems.

Attending conferences provides direct exposure to industry trends and networking opportunities with leading FP practitioners.

Contributing to Open Source Functional Programming Projects

Contributing to open-source projects is one of the best ways to gain real-world FP experience while staying updated with new developments. Some well-known FP projects include:

- **Haskell**
  - *Pandoc*: A document converter written in Haskell.
  - *XMonad*: A tiling window manager.
- **Scala**
  - *Cats*: A library for functional programming abstractions.
  - *ZIO*: A high-performance asynchronous programming framework.
- **Clojure**
  - *Luminus*: A microservices framework.
  - *Datascript*: A functional database implementation.

By contributing to these projects, developers gain hands-on experience and exposure to best practices in FP.

Exploring New Functional Programming Libraries and Tools

New FP libraries and tools are constantly being developed. Keeping track of these innovations helps developers adopt modern techniques in their work. Some notable libraries and tools include:

- **Immutable Data Structures**
  - *Immutable.js* (JavaScript)
  - *Scala Collections* (Scala)
  - *Persistent Data Structures* (Haskell)
- **Functional Reactive Programming (FRP) Frameworks**
  - *RxJS* (JavaScript)
  - *Reactive Streams* (Scala)
  - *Elm Architecture* (Elm)
- **Category Theory-Based Libraries**
  - *Cats (Scala)*
  - *Scalaz (Scala)*
  - *Arrow (Kotlin)*

Experimenting with these libraries enhances a developer's functional programming toolkit.

Engaging with Research Papers and Academic Literature

For those interested in deep theoretical knowledge, reading research papers on functional programming can provide valuable insights. Some good sources include:

- *The Lambda Calculus: Its Syntax and Semantics* by Henk Barendregt
- *Category Theory for Programmers* by Bartosz Milewski
- *Functional Programming with Bananas, Lenses, Envelopes, and Barbed Wire* by Meijer, Fokkinga, and Paterson

Staying connected with academic advancements ensures a comprehensive understanding of FP.

Implementing Functional Programming in Real-World Projects

One of the most effective ways to stay updated is by applying FP techniques to real-world projects. Some ideas include:

- **Building a Functional API**
  Implement an API using Elixir's Phoenix framework or Haskell's Servant.
- **Creating a Functional Web Application**
  Develop a frontend with Elm or a backend with PureScript.
- **Using FP for Data Analysis**
  Write data transformation pipelines in Scala or Haskell.

Practical application of FP principles solidifies knowledge and keeps developers engaged with modern practices.

Conclusion

Staying updated with functional programming advancements requires a multi-faceted approach, combining continuous learning, community engagement, hands-on practice, and exploration of new tools and frameworks. By following blogs, participating in discussions, enrolling in courses, attending conferences, contributing to open-source projects, and applying FP principles in real-world scenarios, developers can ensure they remain at the forefront of functional programming.

Functional programming continues to evolve, shaping the future of software development. Those who actively engage with its advancements will be well-positioned to build high-quality, scalable, and maintainable software systems.

The Role of Functional Programming in AI and Blockchain

Functional programming (FP) is playing an increasingly important role in cutting-edge technologies such as artificial intelligence (AI) and blockchain. The declarative nature, immutability, and higher-order functions inherent in FP make it well-suited for solving the challenges in these domains. This section explores how FP contributes to AI and blockchain, its advantages, and practical implementations in both fields.

Functional Programming in Artificial Intelligence

Artificial intelligence relies on handling vast amounts of data, parallel computations, and mathematical modeling, all of which align well with functional programming principles. Many AI libraries and frameworks incorporate FP features to enhance modularity, performance, and maintainability.

Benefits of Functional Programming in AI

1. **Immutable Data Processing**
   AI models require clean and consistent data. FP's immutable data structures prevent unintended side effects, ensuring that models work with reliable datasets.
2. **Concurrency and Parallelism**
   Training machine learning (ML) models often involves processing large datasets. FP's pure functions enable parallel execution, improving efficiency.
3. **Higher-Order Functions for Data Transformation**
   Data processing in AI frequently involves mapping, filtering, and reducing datasets. FP's built-in support for higher-order functions simplifies these transformations.
4. **Deterministic Computation**
   AI models must produce reproducible results. Pure functions ensure that the same input always results in the same output, which is crucial for debugging and optimizing models.
5. **Lazy Evaluation for Performance Optimization**
   Many FP languages support lazy evaluation, meaning computations are deferred until their results are required. This is useful in AI, where processing massive datasets efficiently is critical.

Functional Programming in Machine Learning

Many popular machine learning libraries and frameworks implement FP concepts to improve model composition and reusability.

Data Transformation with Functional Programming

Before training AI models, data must be preprocessed and cleaned. FP simplifies this through function composition.

Example in Python using functional paradigms for data preprocessing:

```python
from functools import reduce


# Sample dataset
data = [10, 50, 200, 30, 500, 20]


# Functional approach for preprocessing
normalize = lambda x: x / max(data)
remove_outliers = lambda x: x if x < 100 else None
pipeline = lambda data: list(filter(None, map(normalize, data)))


processed_data = pipeline(data)
print(processed_data)  # Normalized data without outliers
```

This approach leverages higher-order functions (map, filter) to make transformations more modular and reusable.

Neural Network Implementation Using Functional Programming

Functional programming makes designing and composing neural networks more intuitive.

Example of a simple neural network implementation using FP concepts:

```python
import numpy as np


# Activation function

relu = lambda x: np.maximum(0, x)


# Forward pass function

def forward_pass(inputs, weights):

    return relu(np.dot(inputs, weights))


# Sample input and weights

inputs = np.array([0.5, 0.2])

weights = np.array([[0.1, 0.4], [0.3, 0.7]])


output = forward_pass(inputs, weights)

print(output)  # Processed output after activation
```

By structuring neural network operations with pure functions, debugging and testing become easier.

Functional Programming in AI Frameworks

Several AI frameworks and libraries incorporate FP principles:

- **TensorFlow & PyTorch**: Use declarative, functional constructs for defining neural networks.
- **Scikit-learn**: Implements functional data transformations (map, reduce).
- **Keras**: Uses function composition for defining deep learning layers.

Functional Programming in Blockchain

Blockchain technology is fundamentally based on cryptographic principles and immutable data structures, making FP a natural fit for developing blockchain applications.

Benefits of Functional Programming in Blockchain

1. **Immutability and Ledger Consistency**
Blockchain relies on immutability to ensure that past transactions cannot be altered. FP's immutable data structures naturally align with this requirement.
2. **Deterministic Smart Contracts**
Smart contracts must execute predictably and without side effects. Pure functions ensure that smart contracts produce consistent outputs.
3. **Concurrency and Distributed Computation**
Blockchains operate in a decentralized environment where multiple nodes validate transactions. FP's support for concurrency enhances performance and security.
4. **Mathematical Soundness**
Blockchain protocols rely on cryptographic proofs and game-theoretic incentives. FP's mathematical foundations provide strong guarantees for correctness.
5. **Security and Formal Verification**
FP languages like Haskell and OCaml facilitate formal verification, which is crucial for securing blockchain applications against vulnerabilities.

Functional Programming in Smart Contracts

Smart contracts define business logic that runs on a blockchain network. FP principles help ensure smart contracts are predictable and secure.

Example: A Simple Smart Contract in Solidity (Using FP Principles)

Although Solidity is not purely functional, FP techniques can be applied:

```
pragma solidity ^0.8.0;


contract Token {

    mapping(address => uint) balances;


    function transfer(address to, uint amount) public {

        require(balances[msg.sender] >= amount, "Insufficient
balance");


        balances[msg.sender] -= amount;
```

```
        balances[to] += amount;

    }


    function balanceOf(address account) public view returns (uint) {

        return balances[account];

    }

}
```

By avoiding global state modifications outside of function scope, we can make contract behavior more predictable.

Functional Programming in Blockchain Protocols

Many blockchain platforms incorporate FP principles:

- **Haskell**   **in**   **Cardano**
  The Cardano blockchain uses Haskell to ensure mathematically provable smart contracts.
- **Michelson**   **in**   **Tezos**
  Tezos smart contracts use a functional stack-based language, Michelson, for verifiability.
- **Ligo**   **for**   **Tezos**
  A functional programming language designed for writing secure Tezos smart contracts.

Functional Programming for Blockchain Consensus Mechanisms

Blockchain consensus mechanisms, such as Proof of Stake (PoS) and Proof of Work (PoW), can be efficiently implemented using FP.

Example: PoW computation in Haskell:

```
import Crypto.Hash.SHA256 (hash)

import Data.ByteString.Char8 (pack)


mineBlock :: String -> Int -> String
```

```
mineBlock dataStr nonce

  | take 4 (show (hash (pack (dataStr ++ show nonce)))) == "0000" =
show nonce

  | otherwise = mineBlock dataStr (nonce + 1)
```

This function recursively computes a nonce that satisfies a proof-of-work condition.

Functional Reactive Programming in Blockchain

Functional Reactive Programming (FRP) is gaining traction in blockchain for handling real-time transactions and event-driven processing.

Example use case:

- **Decentralized Exchanges (DEXs)**: FP principles enable scalable, event-driven trade processing.
- **Supply Chain Management**: Blockchain-based supply chains use FP for immutable ledger tracking.

Challenges of Using Functional Programming in Blockchain and AI

Despite its advantages, FP faces some challenges:

1. **Performance Overhead**: Immutable data structures can be memory-intensive.
2. **Limited Talent Pool**: FP languages are less widely adopted, making hiring skilled developers difficult.
3. **Interoperability**: Many existing AI and blockchain solutions are written in imperative languages.

Conclusion

Functional programming is increasingly shaping the future of AI and blockchain. Its immutability, mathematical soundness, and support for concurrency make it an excellent choice for both domains. AI benefits from FP's deterministic computation and modularity, while blockchain leverages FP for secure, scalable, and verifiable smart contracts.

As these fields continue to evolve, functional programming will play a crucial role in solving emerging challenges, making it an indispensable tool for developers working on AI and blockchain technologies.

Final Thoughts and Next Steps for Mastery

Functional programming (FP) is not just a paradigm—it is a mindset that fundamentally changes how developers think about software. With its emphasis on immutability, pure functions, and declarative code, FP offers a robust approach to writing scalable, maintainable, and bug-resistant applications. As FP continues to influence mainstream programming languages and modern software development, mastering it has become a valuable skill for engineers across all domains.

This section provides final insights on functional programming, best practices for continuous learning, and actionable steps to deepen mastery in FP.

Embracing the Functional Mindset

Shifting to functional programming requires a change in how problems are approached. The key aspects of this mindset include:

1. **Thinking in Functions, Not Objects**
   - Instead of designing objects with mutable states, think about transformations between immutable data structures.
   - Functions become the primary building blocks, composed together to create powerful solutions.
2. **Avoiding Side Effects**
   - Pure functions should always return the same output for the same input.
   - Side effects (I/O, database interactions, state modifications) should be handled explicitly using monads or functional abstractions.
3. **Favoring Immutability**
   - Mutable state leads to unpredictable behaviors and debugging difficulties.
   - Data structures should be immutable, and updates should be handled using persistent data structures.
4. **Leveraging Higher-Order Functions**
   - Functions can accept and return other functions, leading to highly reusable and composable code.
   - Common FP techniques include function composition, currying, and partial application.

Common Pitfalls to Avoid in Functional Programming

Even experienced developers can fall into common traps when transitioning to FP. Some of these include:

- **Misusing Recursion:** While recursion is a powerful FP tool, inefficient use can lead to performance bottlenecks. Tail call optimization (TCO) should be utilized where possible.

Example of improper recursion in JavaScript:

```
function factorial(n) {

    if (n === 0) return 1;
```

```
    return n * factorial(n - 1); // Risk of stack overflow for large
n

}
```

Optimized using tail recursion:

```
function factorial(n, acc = 1) {

    if (n === 0) return acc;

    return factorial(n - 1, acc * n);

}
```

- **Overusing Anonymous Functions:** While lambda functions are useful, excessive nesting can make code unreadable. Prefer named functions when clarity is needed.
- **Ignoring Performance Costs of Immutability:** Creating new objects instead of modifying existing ones can cause memory overhead. Persistent data structures or optimized FP libraries should be considered.

Applying Functional Programming in Real-World Projects

Theoretical knowledge of FP is valuable, but practical application is necessary to achieve mastery. Here are some concrete steps:

1. Start Small with Functional Utilities

- Introduce FP gradually by using higher-order functions such as map, reduce, and filter in daily coding tasks.
- Replace imperative loops with declarative function compositions.

Example: Refactoring imperative code into FP style in Python:

Imperative approach:

```
numbers = [1, 2, 3, 4, 5]

squared_numbers = []

for num in numbers:
```

```
    squared_numbers.append(num ** 2)

print(squared_numbers)
```

Functional approach:

```
squared_numbers = list(map(lambda x: x ** 2, [1, 2, 3, 4, 5]))

print(squared_numbers)
```

2. Build a Small Functional Project

- Create a simple project using a functional-first language such as Haskell, Clojure, or Elixir.
- Implement a calculator, a small API, or a game logic engine using pure functions.

3. Refactor Existing Codebases

- Identify areas in an existing project that rely heavily on mutable state and refactor them using functional constructs.
- Replace classes with function compositions where applicable.

Example: Converting an object-oriented approach to a functional approach in JavaScript:

OOP Approach:

```
class User {

    constructor(name) {

        this.name = name;

    }


    greet() {

        return `Hello, ${this.name}`;

    }
```

```
}
```

Functional Approach:

```javascript
const createUser = (name) => ({

    greet: () => `Hello, ${name}`

});


const user = createUser("Alice");

console.log(user.greet());
```

4. Explore Functional Frameworks and Libraries

- **For Web Development:** Use Elm or PureScript for frontend applications.
- **For Backend Development:** Explore frameworks like Phoenix (Elixir) or Scalatra (Scala).
- **For Data Processing:** Use Apache Spark's functional APIs in Scala or PySpark.

5. Experiment with Functional Reactive Programming (FRP)

- Learn how FP is used in real-time applications like UI frameworks and event-driven architectures.
- Explore RxJS in JavaScript or ReactiveX in Scala/Python.

Leveraging Advanced Functional Programming Concepts

After mastering the basics, exploring advanced FP concepts can deepen understanding:

1. **Algebraic Data Types (ADTs)**
   - Understanding sum types and product types in FP.
   - Example in Haskell:

h

```haskell
data Shape = Circle Float | Rectangle Float Float
```

2.
3. **Monads and Functors**

       ○ Learning how monads handle side effects and enable composition.
       ○ Example of using the `Maybe` monad in Haskell:

haskell

```haskell
safeDivide :: Float -> Float -> Maybe Float

safeDivide _ 0 = Nothing

safeDivide x y = Just (x / y)
```

    4.
    5. **Category Theory for Functional Programmers**
       ○ Learning about monoids, semigroups, and category laws to structure functional programs more effectively.

Engaging with the Functional Programming Community

Continuous learning is easier with community engagement. To stay updated:

- Follow FP blogs and newsletters such as "Lambda the Ultimate" and "Functional Programming Weekly."
- Join FP forums like the r/functionalprogramming subreddit or the Haskell Discourse.
- Attend FP conferences like Lambda Days, Haskell eXchange, and ElixirConf.
- Contribute to FP open-source projects on GitHub.

Final Thoughts

Functional programming is more than just an alternative paradigm—it is a transformative approach to writing clear, scalable, and maintainable software. As languages like JavaScript, Python, and Java continue to adopt FP features, mastering FP concepts will provide an edge in modern software development.

By progressively adopting functional techniques, building real-world projects, and staying engaged with the FP community, developers can unlock the full potential of functional programming. Whether applied to data science, blockchain, AI, or scalable web applications, functional programming is shaping the future of software engineering.

The next step for any aspiring functional programmer is simple: start writing functional code today, experiment with new FP techniques, and embrace the journey toward mastering functional programming.

Chapter 11: Appendices

Glossary of Terms

Functional programming introduces a variety of concepts and terminology that may be unfamiliar to those coming from imperative or object-oriented backgrounds. This glossary provides clear definitions and explanations of key terms used throughout the book, helping readers solidify their understanding of functional programming principles.

A

- **Abstract Data Type (ADT)** – A mathematical model for data structures that defines their behavior but not their implementation. Examples include lists, sets, and maps.
- **Applicative Functor** – A higher-level abstraction than functors that allows function application within a computational context. Commonly used in functional languages to handle computations with side effects.
- **Arity** – The number of arguments a function takes. Functions with a single argument are unary, with two arguments are binary, and so on.
- **Anonymous Function (Lambda)** – A function without a name, often used in functional programming to create short-lived functions for immediate execution.

```
-- Example of an anonymous function in Haskell

(\x -> x * 2) 5   -- Returns 10
```

B

- **Beta Reduction** – The process of applying a function to its arguments in lambda calculus, effectively reducing an expression by replacing function calls with their results.
- **Bound Variable** – A variable whose value is fixed within a given function or scope. Contrasts with free variables, which are not explicitly defined within a function.

C

- **Category Theory** – A branch of mathematics that provides a foundation for functional programming, defining concepts such as functors, monads, and morphisms.
- **Closure** – A function that retains access to its lexical scope, even when executed outside of that scope.

```
// Example of closure in JavaScript
```

```
function counter() {

  let count = 0;

  return function () {

    count++;

    return count;

  };

}


const increment = counter();

console.log(increment()); // 1

console.log(increment()); // 2
```

- **Combinator** – A function with no free variables, meaning it only relies on its input arguments and does not reference variables from an external scope.
- **Currying** – The process of transforming a function that takes multiple arguments into a sequence of functions that each take a single argument.

```
// Currying in Scala

def multiply(a: Int)(b: Int): Int = a * b

val double = multiply(2) _   // Partial application

println(double(5))   // Output: 10
```

D

- **Declarative Programming** – A style of programming that focuses on expressing logic without explicitly defining control flow, commonly used in functional programming.
- **Deterministic Function** – A function that always produces the same output given the same input, without side effects.

E

- **Evaluation Strategy** – The rules governing how function arguments are evaluated. Common strategies include eager evaluation (strict) and lazy evaluation (non-strict).
- **Expression** – A combination of values, variables, and operators that can be evaluated to produce a result. Functional programming emphasizes the use of expressions over statements.

F

- **First-Class Function** – A function that can be assigned to variables, passed as arguments, and returned from other functions.
- **Functor** – A structure that can be mapped over, commonly represented as a type class in functional languages like Haskell and Scala.

```
-- Functor instance for Maybe in Haskell

instance Functor Maybe where

  fmap _ Nothing = Nothing

  fmap f (Just x) = Just (f x)
```

G

- **Generalized Algebraic Data Type (GADT)** – A more powerful form of algebraic data types that allows specifying return types for different constructors.
- **Graph Reduction** – A method of evaluating functional expressions by transforming them into a directed graph and reducing them to their simplest form.

H

- **Higher-Order Function** – A function that takes another function as an argument or returns a function as its result.
- **Hindley-Milner Type System** – A type inference system used in functional programming languages like Haskell, allowing types to be automatically deduced.

```
-- Example of a higher-order function in Haskell

applyTwice :: (a -> a) -> a -> a

applyTwice f x = f (f x)
```

```
applyTwice (*2) 3  -- Output: 12
```

I

- **Immutability** – A key principle in functional programming where data cannot be changed after it is created. Instead, new values are returned when modifications are needed.

```python
# Immutable data structures in Python
from collections import namedtuple

Point = namedtuple("Point", ["x", "y"])
p1 = Point(2, 3)
p2 = p1._replace(x=5)  # Returns a new instance
```

- **Idempotent Function** – A function that produces the same result regardless of how many times it is called with the same inputs.
- **Implicit Parameters** – Parameters that are passed automatically by the compiler, commonly seen in Scala and Haskell.

J

- **Java Functional Interfaces** – Interfaces in Java that contain a single abstract method, enabling functional programming features like lambda expressions.

```java
// Example of a functional interface in Java
@FunctionalInterface
interface MyFunction {
    int apply(int x);
}
```

```
MyFunction square = x -> x * x;

System.out.println(square.apply(4));   // Output: 16
```

L

- **Lazy Evaluation** – A strategy where expressions are not evaluated until their results are actually needed, improving performance in functional languages like Haskell.
- **Lambda Calculus** – A formal system for defining functions and their evaluations, forming the theoretical foundation of functional programming.

M

- **Monads** – A design pattern used to handle side effects in functional programming by wrapping values in a computational context and chaining operations.

```
-- Example of the Maybe monad in Haskell

safeDivide :: Double -> Double -> Maybe Double

safeDivide _ 0 = Nothing

safeDivide x y = Just (x / y)
```

- **Memoization** – A technique for optimizing functions by storing the results of expensive computations and reusing them when the same inputs occur again.

P

- **Pattern Matching** – A mechanism for checking and destructuring values based on their structure, commonly used in functional programming languages.

```
// Pattern matching in Scala

val result = 42 match {

  case 0 => "Zero"

  case 42 => "The answer"
```

```
  case _ => "Something else"

}

println(result)  // Output: "The answer"
```

R

- **Recursion** – A technique where a function calls itself to solve a problem, often replacing loops in functional programming.

```
# Recursive factorial function in Python

def factorial(n):

    return 1 if n == 0 else n * factorial(n - 1)


print(factorial(5))  # Output: 120
```

T

- **Tail Recursion** – A form of recursion where the recursive call is the last operation in a function, allowing optimizations to avoid stack overflow.

This glossary provides a strong reference for understanding the core concepts and terminology of functional programming, serving as a valuable resource for both beginners and experienced developers.

Resources for Further Learning

Functional programming is a deep and evolving field with numerous resources available for learners at all levels. Whether you are a beginner looking to grasp the fundamentals or an advanced developer aiming to refine your expertise, the following categories of resources will guide you through your learning journey.

Books on Functional Programming

Books provide an in-depth understanding of concepts, techniques, and best practices. Below are some highly recommended books on functional programming:

- **"Functional Programming in Scala" by Paul Chiusano and Runar Bjarnason**
  This book introduces functional programming using Scala, covering topics such as immutability, monads, and functional data structures.
- **"Haskell Programming from First Principles" by Christopher Allen and Julie Moronuki**
  A great resource for those who want to learn Haskell from scratch, covering functional concepts in a clear and structured manner.
- **"Structure and Interpretation of Computer Programs" by Harold Abelson and Gerald Jay Sussman**
  Originally used at MIT, this book provides a solid foundation in programming and emphasizes the importance of functional paradigms.
- **"The Little Schemer" by Daniel P. Friedman and Matthias Felleisen**
  A fun and interactive introduction to functional programming using Scheme, teaching recursion and functional thinking.
- **"Purely Functional Data Structures" by Chris Okasaki**
  This book dives into the design of immutable data structures, a crucial aspect of functional programming.

For those looking to explore a broader range of topics, online retailers and publishers such as O'Reilly, Manning, and No Starch Press offer an extensive selection of books on functional programming.

Online Courses and Tutorials

Online courses are an excellent way to learn functional programming interactively. Here are some of the best platforms and courses:

- **Coursera – "Functional Programming in Scala" by École Polytechnique Fédérale de Lausanne (EPFL)**
  This course, taught by Martin Odersky, the creator of Scala, introduces functional programming concepts with practical applications in Scala.
- **edX – "Introduction to Functional Programming" by Delft University of Technology**
  This course covers fundamental principles of functional programming and uses Haskell to demonstrate key concepts.
- **Udemy – "Functional Programming for Beginners"**
  A beginner-friendly introduction to functional programming, covering fundamental principles using JavaScript, Python, and Scala.
- **Frontend Masters – "Hardcore Functional Programming in JavaScript"**
  This advanced course delves into pure functions, immutability, functors, monads, and other functional programming techniques in JavaScript.
- **Haskell MOOC by University of Helsinki**
  A free, self-paced course that provides an extensive introduction to Haskell and its applications.

Academic Papers and Research Articles

For those interested in the theoretical foundations and latest research in functional programming, academic papers can provide deep insights:

- **"Can Programming Be Liberated from the von Neumann Style?" by John Backus**
  This classic paper discusses the limitations of imperative programming and advocates for a functional approach.
- **"Monads for Functional Programming" by Philip Wadler**
  A fundamental paper explaining the role of monads in structuring functional programs.
- **"Why Functional Programming Matters" by John Hughes**
  A highly influential paper that highlights the benefits of functional programming, including modularity and composability.
- **"Lambda Calculus: Its Syntax and Semantics" by Henk Barendregt**
  An academic exploration of the lambda calculus, which forms the basis of functional programming.

Many of these papers are available on platforms like ACM Digital Library, arXiv, and ResearchGate.

Community and Discussion Forums

Engaging with the functional programming community can help learners gain insights, ask questions, and share knowledge. Some of the most active communities include:

- **Haskell-Cafe Mailing List** – A great resource for discussions on Haskell and functional programming research.
- **r/functionalprogramming (Reddit)** – A community dedicated to discussing functional programming concepts and practices.
- **Lambda the Ultimate** – A forum for programming language research and discussions related to functional programming.
- **Stack Overflow** – A valuable Q&A site where developers can ask questions and get answers related to functional programming.

Open-Source Functional Programming Projects

Contributing to open-source projects is one of the best ways to gain real-world experience with functional programming. Some notable projects include:

- **GHC (Glasgow Haskell Compiler)** – The most widely used compiler for Haskell, providing a great opportunity to understand compiler internals.
- **Purescript** – A functional programming language inspired by Haskell, but designed to compile to JavaScript.
- **ScalaZ and Cats** – Libraries for functional programming in Scala, providing tools for working with monads, functors, and applicatives.
- **Elm** – A purely functional language designed for front-end development with excellent compiler error messages.

Functional Programming Blogs and Newsletters

Staying updated with new developments is essential for mastering functional programming. Some recommended blogs and newsletters include:

- **Lambda the Ultimate** (https://lambda-the-ultimate.org/) – A blog dedicated to programming language research.
- **Functional Geekery Podcast** – A podcast featuring interviews with experts in functional programming.
- **Haskell Weekly** (https://haskellweekly.news/) – A newsletter that provides curated content on Haskell and functional programming.
- **FP Complete Blog** – Covers in-depth topics related to functional programming in industry applications.
- **Scott Wlaschin's Blog** (https://fsharpforfunandprofit.com/) – Focuses on functional programming using F#.

Functional Programming in Industry

Many companies are actively using functional programming in their products. Exploring case studies can provide insights into real-world applications:

- **Facebook** – Uses functional programming in React, which follows principles of immutability and pure functions.
- **Twitter** – Uses Scala extensively for its backend systems.
- **Jane Street** – A financial firm known for its heavy use of OCaml.
- **Netflix** – Uses functional programming techniques in its recommendation systems and microservices.

Functional Programming Meetups and Conferences

Attending conferences and meetups is a great way to network with functional programming experts:

- **LambdaConf** – One of the biggest conferences focused on functional programming.
- **Functional Conf** – A conference dedicated to the application of functional programming in industry.
- **Haskell eXchange** – A yearly event bringing together Haskell enthusiasts.
- **Curry On** – A conference exploring programming language research and functional programming applications.
- **Local Meetups (via Meetup.com)** – Many cities have functional programming meetup groups where developers can learn and collaborate.

Building Your Own Functional Programming Roadmap

To effectively learn functional programming, it's essential to create a structured learning roadmap. A recommended roadmap is as follows:

1. **Start with the Basics** – Learn about pure functions, immutability, and first-class functions using a beginner-friendly language like JavaScript or Python.
2. **Explore Functional Constructs** – Study concepts such as higher-order functions, function composition, currying, and recursion.
3. **Understand Type Systems** – Learn about static typing and type inference in functional languages like Haskell or Scala.
4. **Dive into Monads and Functors** – Grasp the power of abstract data types and their applications in handling side effects.
5. **Work on Real-World Projects** – Apply functional programming principles by building projects or contributing to open-source software.
6. **Continue Learning and Engaging** – Join functional programming communities, attend conferences, and read academic papers to stay up-to-date.

By leveraging these resources, learners can develop a solid foundation in functional programming and gain the skills necessary to apply it effectively in real-world applications.

Sample Projects and Code Snippets

Functional programming is best learned through hands-on experience. This section provides a series of sample projects and code snippets that illustrate the key concepts of functional programming, ranging from basic principles to more advanced applications. These projects are designed to be language-agnostic, but examples will be provided in commonly used functional programming languages such as Haskell, Scala, JavaScript, and Python.

Project 1: Implementing a Functional Calculator

A functional calculator can be built using pure functions, immutability, and higher-order functions.

Requirements:

- Support basic arithmetic operations (+, -, *, /)
- Support function composition
- Use recursion for handling nested operations

Implementation in Haskell:

```haskell
type Operator = Double -> Double -> Double


add :: Operator

add x y = x + y
```

```haskell
subtract' :: Operator
subtract' x y = x - y


multiply :: Operator
multiply x y = x * y


divide :: Operator
divide _ 0 = error "Cannot divide by zero"
divide x y = x / y


calculate :: Operator -> Double -> Double -> Double
calculate op x y = op x y


main :: IO ()
main = do
    print $ calculate add 10 5        -- Output: 15
    print $ calculate subtract' 10 5 -- Output: 5
    print $ calculate multiply 10 5   -- Output: 50
    print $ calculate divide 10 5     -- Output: 2
```

This implementation ensures that every function is pure and reusable.

Project 2: Functional To-Do List

A to-do list is a common beginner-friendly project. The functional approach involves immutability, recursion, and higher-order functions.

Requirements:

- Add new tasks
- Remove completed tasks
- Display all tasks

Implementation in JavaScript:

```javascript
const addTask = (tasks, task) => [...tasks, task];


const removeTask = (tasks, index) =>
  tasks.filter((_, i) => i !== index);


const displayTasks = (tasks) =>
  tasks.forEach((task,  index)  =>  console.log(`${index  +  1}.
${task}`));


// Example usage:

let tasks = [];

tasks = addTask(tasks, "Learn Functional Programming");

tasks = addTask(tasks, "Write Code in Haskell");

tasks = addTask(tasks, "Read about Monads");


console.log("To-Do List:");

displayTasks(tasks);


tasks = removeTask(tasks, 1);
```

```
console.log("Updated To-Do List:");

displayTasks(tasks);
```

This example uses **immutability** by returning new arrays instead of modifying existing ones.

Project 3: Fibonacci Sequence with Memoization

Memoization optimizes recursive functions by caching results to prevent redundant calculations.

Implementation in Python:

```
from functools import lru_cache


@lru_cache(maxsize=None)

def fibonacci(n):

    if n in (0, 1):

        return n

    return fibonacci(n - 1) + fibonacci(n - 2)


print([fibonacci(n) for n in range(10)])
```

Using `@lru_cache`, we ensure that previously computed Fibonacci numbers are stored, reducing time complexity from O(2^n) to O(n).

Project 4: Functional Data Processing Pipeline

Data processing is a common real-world application of functional programming. This example demonstrates how to transform a dataset using pure functions and pipelines.

Requirements:

- Filter out invalid data
- Transform data to uppercase
- Sort data alphabetically

Implementation in Scala:

```scala
object FunctionalPipeline extends App {

  val names = List("Alice", "bob", "", "CHARLIE", "dave", "")


  val cleanData = (data: List[String]) => data.filter(_.nonEmpty)

  val transformData = (data: List[String]) => data.map(_.toUpperCase)

  val sortData = (data: List[String]) => data.sorted


  val processData = cleanData andThen transformData andThen sortData


  println(processData(names))
}
```

This example demonstrates **function composition** using andThen, making the code modular and expressive.

Project 5: Implementing a Custom Lazy Evaluation Mechanism

Lazy evaluation allows computations to be deferred until needed. This technique is useful for optimizing performance.

Implementation in JavaScript:

```javascript
const lazy = (fn) => {
```

```
let computed = false;

let result;


return () => {

  if (!computed) {

    result = fn();

    computed = true;

  }

  return result;

};

};


const expensiveComputation = lazy(() => {

  console.log("Computing...");

  return 42;

});


console.log(expensiveComputation()); // "Computing..." then 42

console.log(expensiveComputation()); // 42 (cached result)
```

This example ensures that expensiveComputation is only executed once and then cached for future use.

Project 6: Functional Error Handling with Option Type

Functional programming often avoids exceptions by using algebraic data types like `Option` to handle errors safely.

Implementation in Haskell:

```haskell
data Option a = Some a | None deriving (Show)

safeDivide :: Double -> Double -> Option Double

safeDivide _ 0 = None

safeDivide x y = Some (x / y)


main :: IO ()

main = do

    print $ safeDivide 10 2 -- Some 5.0

    print $ safeDivide 10 0 -- None
```

This pattern prevents runtime exceptions and makes error handling explicit.

Project 7: Functional Logging System

A logging system that maintains immutability and pure functions while logging messages.

Implementation in Python:

```python
def log_message(logs, message):

    return logs + [message]


def display_logs(logs):
```

```python
    for log in logs:

        print(log)


logs = []

logs = log_message(logs, "Started application")

logs = log_message(logs, "User logged in")

logs = log_message(logs, "Error: Invalid input")


display_logs(logs)
```

This approach avoids modifying a shared state and maintains immutability.

Project 8: Implementing Functional State Management

State is often handled imperatively, but in functional programming, immutable data structures and pure functions are preferred.

Implementation in JavaScript:

```javascript
const updateState = (state, updates) => ({ ...state, ...updates });


let state = { user: "Alice", loggedIn: false };

state = updateState(state, { loggedIn: true });


console.log(state); // { user: "Alice", loggedIn: true }
```

This method ensures **immutability** and prevents unintended side effects.

Conclusion

These sample projects demonstrate key principles of functional programming, including immutability, pure functions, function composition, lazy evaluation, and error handling. By applying these concepts, developers can write more predictable, maintainable, and efficient software. Functional programming encourages thinking in terms of transformations rather than state changes, resulting in cleaner and more modular code.

For further learning, readers are encouraged to modify and extend these projects or implement them in different functional programming languages.

API Reference Guide

This section provides an API reference guide for core functional programming utilities and constructs. It includes commonly used functions, data structures, and concepts, illustrated with practical examples in functional programming languages such as Haskell, Scala, JavaScript, and Python.

1. Pure Functions

A **pure function** is one that always produces the same output given the same input and has no side effects.

Definition:

- Deterministic (output depends only on input)
- No external state modification
- No reliance on external variables

Example in JavaScript:

```
const add = (x, y) => x + y;

console.log(add(2, 3)); // Output: 5
```

2. Higher-Order Functions

A **higher-order function** is a function that takes another function as an argument or returns a function as a result.

Example in Python:

```python
def apply_function(func, value):

    return func(value)


double = lambda x: x * 2

print(apply_function(double, 5))  # Output: 10
```

---

3. Function Composition

Function composition allows small functions to be combined into more complex ones.

Example in Haskell:

```haskell
double :: Int -> Int
double x = x * 2


increment :: Int -> Int
increment x = x + 1


compose :: (b -> c) -> (a -> b) -> (a -> c)
compose f g x = f (g x)


main = print (compose double increment 3)  -- Output: 8
```

---

4. Currying and Partial Application

Currying transforms a function with multiple arguments into a sequence of functions, each taking one argument.

Example in Scala:

```
def multiply(a: Int)(b: Int): Int = a * b

val double = multiply(2) _



println(double(5))   // Output: 10
```

---

5. Immutability

Functional programming avoids mutable state. Instead of modifying existing structures, new ones are created.

Example in JavaScript:

```
const addElement = (arr, element) => [...arr, element];


const numbers = [1, 2, 3];

const newNumbers = addElement(numbers, 4);


console.log(newNumbers);   // Output: [1, 2, 3, 4]
```

---

6. Lazy Evaluation

Lazy evaluation delays computation until the result is required.

Example in Python:

```python
def lazy_range(n):

    for i in range(n):

        yield i


numbers = lazy_range(5)

print(next(numbers))   # Output: 0

print(next(numbers))   # Output: 1
```

---

7. Algebraic Data Types (ADTs)

ADTs define complex data structures by composing simpler types.

Example in Haskell:

```haskell
data Maybe a = Nothing | Just a deriving Show


safeDivide :: Double -> Double -> Maybe Double

safeDivide _ 0 = Nothing

safeDivide x y = Just (x / y)


main = print (safeDivide 10 2)   -- Output: Just 5.0
```

---

8. Pattern Matching

Pattern matching simplifies function definitions and conditional logic.

Example in Scala:

```scala
def matchNumber(n: Int): String = n match {

  case 1 => "One"

  case 2 => "Two"

  case _ => "Other"

}



println(matchNumber(2))  // Output: "Two"
```

---

9. Functors and Monads

A **functor** applies a function to a wrapped value. A **monad** extends functors by handling computation sequencing.

Example in Haskell (Functor):

```haskell
instance Functor Maybe where

  fmap _ Nothing = Nothing

  fmap f (Just x) = Just (f x)



main = print (fmap (*2) (Just 3))  -- Output: Just 6
```

Example in Haskell (Monad):

```haskell
safeDivide :: Double -> Double -> Maybe Double
```

```
safeDivide _ 0 = Nothing

safeDivide x y = Just (x / y)



main = print (Just 10 >>= (`safeDivide` 2))   -- Output: Just 5.0
```

---

10. Functional Error Handling

Instead of using exceptions, functional programming relies on monadic types like Option, Either, and Try.

Example in Scala (Option):

```
def safeDivide(x: Int, y: Int): Option[Int] =
  if (y == 0) None else Some(x / y)


println(safeDivide(10, 2))  // Output: Some(5)

println(safeDivide(10, 0))  // Output: None
```

---

11. Streams and Pipelines

Streams allow for functional transformations on sequences of data.

Example in JavaScript:

```
const numbers = [1, 2, 3, 4, 5];


const processed = numbers
```

```
.map(n => n * 2)

.filter(n => n > 5);
```

```
console.log(processed);    // Output: [6, 8, 10]
```

12. Functional Reactive Programming (FRP)

FRP models systems as streams of events rather than state changes.

Example in RxJS (JavaScript):

```
const { fromEvent } = require('rxjs');

const { map } = require('rxjs/operators');
```

```
const clicks = fromEvent(document, 'click');

const positions = clicks.pipe(map(event => event.clientX));
```

```
positions.subscribe(x => console.log(x));
```

13. State Management in Functional Programming

Managing state functionally involves passing state explicitly rather than modifying global variables.

Example in JavaScript:

```
const updateState = (state, update) => ({ ...state, ...update });
```

```
let state = { user: "Alice", loggedIn: false };

state = updateState(state, { loggedIn: true });


console.log(state); // { user: "Alice", loggedIn: true }
```

---

14. Functional Programming in Web Development

Functional programming principles can be applied in front-end frameworks like React.

Example in React (JavaScript):

```
import { useState } from 'react';


function Counter() {

  const [count, setCount] = useState(0);

  return (

    <div>

      <p>Count: {count}</p>

      <button onClick={() => setCount(count + 1)}>Increment</button>

    </div>

  );

}
```

---

15. Functional Programming in Data Science

Functional programming enhances data science workflows by ensuring immutability and function composition.

Example in Python (Pandas Functional Approach):

```
import pandas as pd


df = pd.DataFrame({'A': [1, 2, 3], 'B': [4, 5, 6]})

df_transformed = df.assign(A=df["A"] * 2, B=df["B"] + 1)


print(df_transformed)
```

Conclusion

This API reference guide provides a comprehensive overview of functional programming principles and their practical applications. By leveraging immutability, higher-order functions, monads, and function composition, developers can write modular, efficient, and maintainable software. This guide serves as a reference for building functional applications and improving functional programming proficiency.

Frequently Asked Questions

This section addresses common questions related to functional programming, covering fundamental concepts, practical applications, and best practices. Whether you are a beginner or an experienced developer, these answers will help clarify key aspects of functional programming.

General Questions

What is functional programming?

Functional programming is a programming paradigm that treats computation as the evaluation of mathematical functions while avoiding changing state and mutable data. It emphasizes:

- **Pure functions** (no side effects)

- **Immutability** (data cannot be changed after creation)
- **First-class and higher-order functions** (functions can be assigned to variables, passed as arguments, and returned from other functions)
- **Function composition** (small functions can be combined to create complex behavior)

How is functional programming different from imperative programming?

Feature	Functional Programming	Imperative Programming
State Management	Immutable state	Mutable state
Control Flow	Expression-based	Statement-based
Side Effects	Avoided	Often present
Function Usage	First-class, higher-order	Often procedural
Example Languages	Haskell, Scala, Clojure	Java, C, Python (OO)

In functional programming, you describe *what* to do, whereas imperative programming focuses on *how* to do it.

Is functional programming better than object-oriented programming?

Both paradigms have their strengths.

- **Functional programming** is best suited for stateless, data-driven applications such as data transformation pipelines, parallel computing, and distributed systems.
- **Object-oriented programming (OOP)** excels in modeling real-world entities, encapsulating behavior, and managing complex stateful systems.

Many modern applications combine both paradigms to leverage their advantages.

Conceptual Questions

What are pure functions? Why are they important?

A **pure function** is a function where:

1. The output depends only on the input.
2. It has no side effects (does not modify external state).

Example in JavaScript:

```javascript
const add = (x, y) => x + y;

console.log(add(3, 5));  // Output: 8
```

Since add does not modify external variables or rely on anything other than its inputs, it is **pure**.

Benefits of pure functions:

- **Predictability:** Always returns the same result for the same input.
- **Easier testing:** No hidden dependencies.
- **Parallelism-friendly:** Since there are no side effects, functions can run concurrently.

What is immutability? Why is it useful?

Immutability means that once a value is created, it cannot be changed. Instead of modifying existing data, new data structures are returned.

Example in Python (Immutable Lists with Tuples):

```python
immutable_list = (1, 2, 3)

new_list = immutable_list + (4,)   # Creates a new tuple instead of modifying the original

print(new_list)  # Output: (1, 2, 3, 4)
```

Benefits:

- **Avoids unintended modifications** (no accidental state changes).
- **Easier debugging** (values never change unpredictably).

- **Thread-safe computations** (suitable for concurrent programming).

Practical Questions

What is function composition? How is it different from method chaining?

Function composition is the process of combining small functions into larger ones.

Example in Haskell:

```haskell
double :: Int -> Int
double x = x * 2


increment :: Int -> Int
increment x = x + 1


composedFunction :: Int -> Int
composedFunction = double . increment   -- Composition


main = print (composedFunction 3)   -- Output: 8
```

Method chaining (common in OOP) involves calling multiple methods sequentially on an object.

Example in JavaScript:

```javascript
const result = [1, 2, 3]
  .map(x => x * 2)
  .filter(x => x > 3)
  .reduce((a, b) => a + b, 0);
```

```
console.log(result);   // Output: 10
```

Both techniques achieve similar goals, but function composition is more **declarative** and aligns with **mathematical reasoning**.

What are monads? Do I really need to understand them?

A **monad** is a design pattern that represents computations as a sequence of steps. It is used to **handle side effects** like IO, state, or exceptions while keeping code **pure**.

Example in Haskell (Maybe Monad for Safe Division):

```
safeDivide :: Double -> Double -> Maybe Double

safeDivide _ 0 = Nothing

safeDivide x y = Just (x / y)



main = print (safeDivide 10 2)   -- Output: Just 5.0
```

Do you need to understand them?

- If you are using functional programming professionally (Haskell, Scala, F#), **yes**.
- If you are using functional techniques in JavaScript, Python, or Java, **not necessarily**, but understanding monads helps with handling **async operations** (like Promises in JavaScript).

How does functional programming handle errors without exceptions?

Functional programming avoids exceptions using **algebraic data types (ADTs)** such as:

- Option (Scala) or Maybe (Haskell) for handling missing values.
- Either (Scala, Haskell) for representing success (Right) or failure (Left).

Example in Scala (Either for Error Handling):

```
def safeDivide(x: Double, y: Double): Either[String, Double] =

  if (y == 0) Left("Cannot divide by zero") else Right(x / y)


println(safeDivide(10, 2))   // Output: Right(5.0)

println(safeDivide(10, 0))   // Output: Left("Cannot divide by zero")
```

This ensures errors are **explicitly handled** rather than relying on **try/catch**.

Industry and Performance Questions

Where is functional programming used in the real world?

Functional programming is widely used in:

- **Web development** – React.js, Elm
- **Data science** – Apache Spark (Scala)
- **Finance** – Jane Street uses OCaml for trading systems
- **Machine learning** – TensorFlow uses functional techniques
- **Distributed computing** – Akka (Scala), Erlang

Companies like Facebook, Twitter, Netflix, and Uber utilize functional programming for **scalability** and **fault tolerance**.

Is functional programming slow?

Functional programming emphasizes immutability, which can increase memory usage. However, **optimizations** like:

- **Lazy evaluation** (Haskell)
- **Persistent data structures** (Clojure, Scala)
- **Tail call optimization** (Eliminates stack overflow issues in recursion)

ensure that functional code is **efficient** in real-world applications.

Getting Started

How should I start learning functional programming?

1. **Choose a language** – JavaScript, Python, or Haskell.
2. **Understand core principles** – Pure functions, immutability, function composition.
3. **Solve problems functionally** – Practice with recursion and higher-order functions.
4. **Learn about monads and ADTs** (optional, for advanced use cases).
5. **Work on a project** – Build a functional API, data processing pipeline, or web application.

Conclusion

Functional programming provides a powerful paradigm for writing **reliable, modular, and scalable** applications. While the learning curve can be steep, adopting its principles leads to **better software design** and **fewer bugs**. By applying the concepts in this FAQ, developers can transition smoothly into **writing functional code** in both **pure FP languages** and **hybrid paradigms** like JavaScript and Python.